HAPPY BY DESIGN

A Guide to Architecture and Mental Wellbeing

D1612975

BEN CHANNON

© RIBA Publishing, 2018

Published by RIBA Publishing, 66 Portland Place, London, W1B 1NT

ISBN 978-1-85946-878-4

British Library Cataloguing-in-Publication Data

A catalogue record for this book is available from the British Library.

Commissioning Editor: Ginny Mills
Project Editor: Daniel Culver
Production & Typesetting: Richard Blackburn
Designed by Ben Channon
Printed and bound by W&G Baird, Great Britain
Author photo by Philippa Gedge
All other images created by Ben Channon

Twitter: @MindfulArchi
Instagram: @happybydesignbook

www.ribapublishing.com

CONTENTS

ACKNOWLEDGEMENTS

As this was my first book, I have relied upon a number of very patient and helpful people throughout the writing process, during which I am sure I have been extremely hard work.

Thank you to all of my colleagues at Assael Architecture for their input, feedback and encouragement.

Thank you also to the wonderful people at the Mindfulness Association, who not only coached me to become a mindfulness practitioner but discussed the idea of this book with me when it was just coming into existence.

I would like to thank my secondary school art teachers David Reshad and George Davis, who convinced me I could actually draw when I thought I was terrible.

I am incredibly grateful to Freddie Daley at Blackstock PR and Ginny Mills at RIBA Publishing for helping me turn this book into an actual, real 'thing' – without them it would just be a file in a badly organised folder on my laptop.

Finally, I would like to thank my family (who are awesome) and my girlfriend Alex (who is also awesome) for putting up with me (and not just while I've been writing this book). Thanks Mum and Dad for encouraging all of my ideas over the years, the good ones and the terrible ones. I hope this turns out to be one of the good ones.

ABOUT THE AUTHOR

Ben Channon is an architect at Assael Architecture, where he has worked since 2012. He is the Mental Wellbeing Ambassador at the practice, which has been praised by the *Architects' Journal* for its approach to staff care. He is an accredited mindfulness practitioner with the Mindfulness Association, and coaches mindfulness at the practice and in his free time.

Ben founded and chairs the Architects' Mental Wellbeing Forum, which is focused on improving mental health within the industry. He has also lectured on wellbeing and architecture at Liverpool University, and writes for a number of publications on this subject.

INTRODUCTION

Welcome to *Happy by Design*. This is a pocket-sized guide to designing buildings that can make people happier. It has been written to be accessible to all – not just architects and designers. Whether you're in the construction industry, are thinking of renovating your own home or redesigning your garden, or are simply interested in finding out how the built environment influences our minds, this book will change the way you think about design.

Since the Ancient Greek 'master builders' we have been obsessed with how people experience buildings, and with good reason: they have a huge impact on how we feel. This interest in human experience was evident in the work of early 20th-century architects such as Le Corbusier, who, in his 1923 book *Towards a New Architecture*, wrote, 'But suddenly you touch my heart, you do me good. I am happy and I say: "This is beautiful".'

I began the journey of writing this book with the realisation that actually much of the construction industry in the 21st century is focused on three things completely unrelated to the experience of buildings: carbon emissions, safety and profits. All of these elements are, of course, important. However, if we focus too heavily on them, it is possible to lose sight of something that should be at the core of design: *joy*.

By most estimations, we now spend more than 80% of our time in buildings, and this can affect our mood both positively and negatively. The quality of the places where we live, work and study therefore impacts our happiness significantly.

People are, by their very definition, 'only human'. From time to time we all find excuses not to go to the gym, make our bed or do the dishes, despite knowing full well that in the long run this will have a negative impact on our happiness. Designers of the built environment have an opportunity to impact our 'human' behaviour in a positive way: to nudge people to exercise or to make it easier to be tidy, for example.

Happiness is an incredibly important but often overlooked aspect of our lives. It can result in improved productivity in the workplace and better learning in students; most importantly, it can drastically improve people's quality of life and physical and mental health.

I became interested in the idea of happiness following some mental health-related issues in my own family. With further research, I discovered that one in four people in the UK suffers from a diagnosable mental health issue. The World Health Organization recently reported that depression is now the leading cause of disability and ill-health worldwide. Discovering the magnitude of this problem inspired me to study with the Mindfulness Association and Mental Health First Aid UK and to create a mental wellbeing programme at the architecture practice where I work.

Mindfulness, at its core, is a meditation-based practice that relies on the simple act of focus, typically on breathing or physical sensations. Practising these exercises daily can cause an actual physical change: a reduction in parts of the brain related to stress and anxiety. MRI scans show that after an eight-week course of mindfulness practice, the brain's 'fight or flight' centre, the amygdala, appears to shrink. However, at a conceptual level it is also about learning how to focus on what is happening in each moment and to experience our surroundings rather than being lost in our thoughts – something that relates closely to the design of places.

Mindfulness has taught me that, while we are all different, there are certain aspects of the human condition that we all have in common. We all eat, we all drink, and we all experience a broadly similar range of emotions.

Buildings also affect us all in largely similar ways. Of course, some people might prefer certain colours or materials, but while researching this book I discovered that there are many elements to building design that will universally affect how people feel within a space.

These fundamental design elements make up the seven sections of this book. The broad categories are closely interlinked, and many of the design tips found in this book could apply across several of the chapters. Where this is the case, symbols for the other relevant categories are featured next to the design tip. Each section is also colour-coded for ease of reference.

Finally, a successful building does not have to include every single one of these tips, but many will be relevant to whatever type of room or building you are designing. At the back of this book you can find an example of a 'happy house', which incorporates many of them.

Whether you are an architect, a designer, a student, a renovator, a developer or a DIYer, feel free to pick and choose the ideas that are most relevant to your project or concept. Including even one of these features will have a positive impact on the mental wellbeing of the people using your space.

1: LIGHT

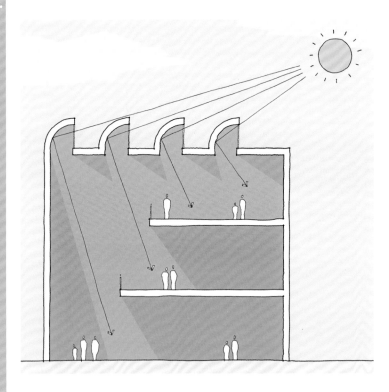

Natural daylight is one of the most fundamental human needs. Its significant impact on human happiness and on our mental wellbeing is well proven through research and data. For example, staff in offices with no natural daylight have been shown to sleep on average 46 minutes less than their light-receiving counterparts.

Daylight affects a number of our basic systems, such as the circadian rhythm – our biological clock – which regulates the timing of periods of sleepiness and wakefulness throughout the day. These systems are sensitively balanced, and even small changes in the amount of daylight we receive can have substantial impacts on our mood, productivity and overall wellbeing. Although artificial lighting is becoming more advanced in how it can mimic the effects of daylight, it is still no substitute for the real thing.

When designing buildings, it is therefore extremely important to consider how you can improve both the quantity and quality of daylight, internally and within landscaping. However, you must also be aware of a range of other factors such as heat gains (or losses) from glazing, and views into and out of buildings.

Orient buildings sensitively

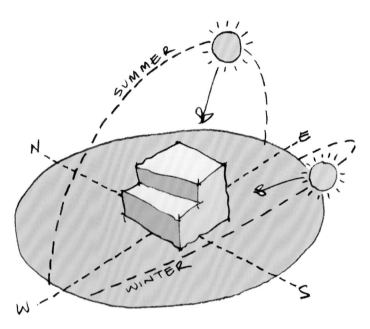

*To maximise solar gains, windows should be orientated within 15°
of true south*

When thinking about the form and layout of a building, daylight should be considered at an early stage. A building's massing and orientation is integral to how much light each space will receive, and which areas will be overshadowed.

While southern-facing rooms will receive the most sunlight (in the northern hemisphere), consider also the impact and qualities of light at certain times of the day. If a space would benefit more from morning light then provide windows facing eastwards.

North-facing windows will receive the least sunlight and therefore spaces that only have a northerly aspect should generally be avoided if possible. Spaces such as libraries or galleries are the exception, where direct sunlight can often damage books or displays.

Consider shadows

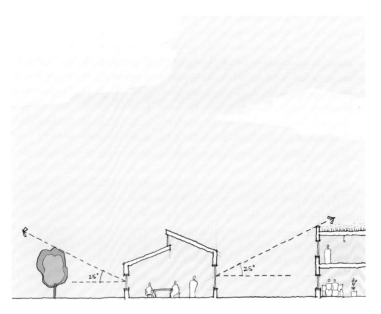

Aim for an angle of greater than 25° as a rule of thumb for good daylighting

One of the earliest decisions about a new building is where to locate it on the site. When undertaking this process, remember the importance of shadows. These can dramatically reduce the amount of daylight and sunlight that key spaces will receive. Consider shadows that might be cast by:

- Neighbouring buildings
- Nearby trees or foliage
- Other elements of your own building

Be selective about window sizes

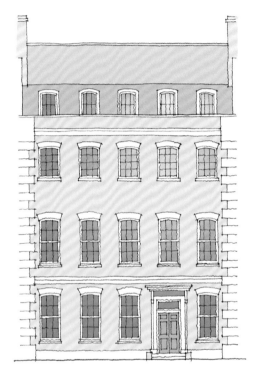

Windows on upper storeys get more daylight, as a result of the increased amount of visible sky

An obvious way to increase the amount of daylight and sunlight within a space is to increase the amount of glazing. However, glass is an expensive material, and also brings with it a range of other issues such as solar gains or thermal losses.

The size of windows should therefore be considered carefully. If budget is an important constraint, decide which spaces will benefit most from the extra daylight they will receive from larger windows.

Remember also that windows higher up a building will receive more daylight than windows on lower floors, as more open sky is visible. This is why many buildings have smaller windows on higher floors.

Avoid deep plans

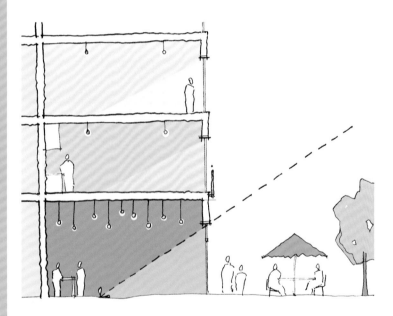

Vitruvius recommended that maximum room depth should be four to five times the height of windows, although modern rules of thumb generally suggest a factor between 2 and 2.5

It is often desirable to design a building to have rooms with a greater depth, known as a 'deep plan'. This can be used to increase the internal area of a building, or to reduce the ratio of facade to floor area and therefore reduce construction costs.

However, by designing in this way you are at risk of creating dark areas at the back of rooms that will rely on artificial lighting. This is not only worse from an energy perspective but will also result in unhappier building occupants. To avoid this, make rooms either shallower or taller.

Use high-level windows to combine light and privacy

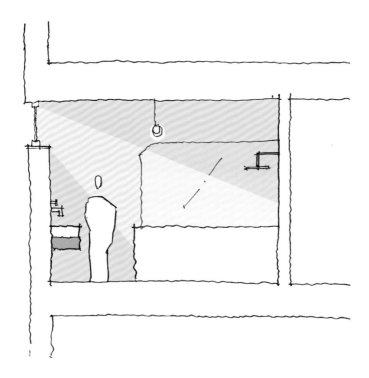

Spaces with no natural daylight provide us with no reference to the outside world, and can be disorienting and even distressing

Although increased daylight in buildings is shown to improve people's mental wellbeing, it is not always desirable to have large windows looking onto private spaces such as bathrooms or changing rooms. As a result, these often end up with no natural daylight at all, giving no view of the sky or reference for our body clocks.

In these instances, a compromise can be easily reached, however. Where possible, try to provide high-level windows that don't permit views in from neighbouring properties. If this is not possible, consider larger windows with opaque glazing, which can even be post-applied to existing windows in the form of a film.

Use rooflights shrewdly

Rooflights can bring in up to twice as much daylight as vertical windows

While rooflights should never be viewed as a direct substitute for traditional windows, they do have certain advantages.

They can be an extremely effective way of bringing light into spaces with limited opportunities for normal windows, and views of the sky can provide a reference to the time of day and the weather. They can also be used to great effect to pick out key parts of a space or to create a powerful sense of drama, as shown in Vector Architects' Seashore Chapel, opposite.

However, as will be discussed later in this book, views outwards offer many other benefits in terms of mental wellbeing. As a result, traditional windows are usually preferable.

Don't overlook artificial light

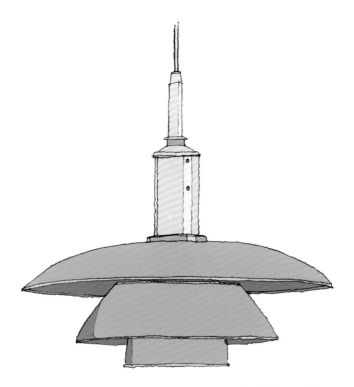

Indirect light has been shown to improve productivity and alertness

Although it is important for designers to get the natural daylight correct, there are also happiness and wellbeing benefits to be gained from good use of artificial lighting.

Danish lighting designer Poul Henningsen devoted much of his career to designing glare-free and uniform illumination, which has been shown to reduce headaches and improve productivity. Studies suggest that emotions are experienced more intensely under bright, harsh lighting, which can have a negative impact on our moods.

Where possible designers should therefore look to avoid direct light or glare from bulbs through uplighting or reflected light, and give users control with dimmers to help create calmer lighting.

Consider the temperature of artificial light

Studies have shown that a low colour temperature triggers the production and release of melatonin, which causes us to relax

When choosing lighting, it is extremely important to think about the use of the space and ensure, the correct temperature bulb is chosen.

Artificial lighting temperatures range from warm 'soft whites' (2700–3000K) to 'bright or cool whites' (3500–4100K) and finally 'daylight' (5000–6500K). Each temperature range creates a different effect and can impact our mood in a variety of ways.

Soft whites create a warm, cosy feeling. These work well in bedrooms and living rooms as they are calming and can help to us to relax, which is key to our mental wellbeing.

Bright and cool whites work best in bathrooms and kitchens. They create a more energetic feeling and help to give better contrast between colours. This increases further as you move towards daylight temperatures; however, these colder shades can impact sleep and begin to feel sterile – perhaps unsurprising given their use in hospitals – so avoid them in spaces where relaxation is desirable.

Use artificial light to create pockets of calm

Quiet alone time is shown to help our brains reboot and unwind, allowing us to think more clearly

Artificial light can be a fantastic way to create a sense of privacy or escapism. While it often tempting as a designer to light all areas brightly and evenly, being selective in where you light can be far more effective.

As with daylight, strategically placed light sources can help to highlight specific areas where people may wish to retreat to read, study or simply relax. This need for quiet escapism is vital to many people, and its effect on our moods is discussed later in this book.

2: COMFORT

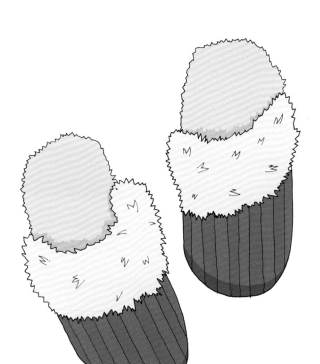

We are all acutely aware of how unpleasant it is to be in a state of discomfort. However, in an age where mass production, low-cost materials and image-based advertising are prevalent, comfort is now only one of a large number of considerations within the design of both furniture and buildings.

We often talk of the importance of being 'comfortable in our own skin', and the philosophy of mindfulness embodies this ideal, arguing that happiness will come through active engagement with our own physical sensations. If we are uncomfortable, we are far less likely to want to engage with our bodies and we therefore tend to switch off from the physical world, which can be detrimental to our mental wellbeing.

Comfort also plays a vital role in helping us to relax and feel calm and safe, all of which are key to happiness. It is therefore hugely important that designers engage with creating comfortable environments.

Use tactile materials

Touch is our most fundamental sense, and is shown to be closely linked to our emotions

Most people can relate to the pleasant sensations of warm sand on our feet, or cool, soft linen bedsheets on our bodies. These tactile materials encourage us to engage directly with our physical sense of touch, which is often overlooked despite its importance. This can help us to focus us on the present moment, which is shown to be beneficial to our mental wellbeing and is a key principle of mindfulness.

This effect can also be created through the use of tactile materials within architectural design, for example with real timber floorboards or exposed brickwork. At a time when cost constraints are leading to the widespread use of plain finishes such as non-natural flooring and plasterboard, more textural materials are to be encouraged wherever possible.

When the budget has been a constraint, many designers have taken to using cheap materials in unlikely ways, for example upcycled timber as a wall finish, or recycled bottle caps within resin as a flooring material. This element of surprise can encourage us to engage with our sense of touch as much as the finest travertine.

Consider comfort as well as aesthetics

Furniture must be fit for purpose as well as visually appealing

It is often tempting when designing a house, hotel or office to choose the most visually appealing furniture, but this should not come at the expense of the way we feel when using it. Being comfortable is an extremely important part of being happy, and this is further heightened when we spend most of our day sitting in an office chair (as many of us do), and night lying in a bed (as almost all of us do).

Furniture must therefore be 'fit for purpose', which in this case means helping us to feel relaxed and enjoy engaging with our bodies. Chairs must support our legs and backs to prevent chronic injury, which is a major cause of depression. Beds must help us to sleep better. As Gloria Hunniford famously said, 'Always buy a good pair of shoes and a good bed, as if you aren't in one you're in the other.'

Sleep plays an enormous role in our happiness and mental health: poor sleep is directly linked to anxiety and depression. Entire nights without sleep are particularly damaging and ironically often lead to anxiety about sleep in the following days, which can in turn cause insomnia. For this reason our sleeping environment is one of the most important areas to focus on when trying to improve people's happiness, and is one that appears frequently within this book. While there are many factors that affect our sleep, a good bed is a great starting point.

Think about the temperature of buildings

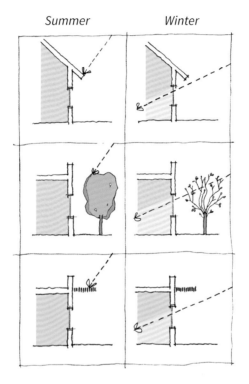

Summer   *Winter*

Ideal summer temperatures for schools, homes and offices are between 21°C and 25°C

Almost everybody reading this book will be able to remember a time when they have felt intensely unhappy due to being too cold or too hot. The temperature of spaces should therefore be considered very early on in the design process.

There are far too many factors affecting building temperatures to name in this short section; however, some general rules of thumb apply. In warmer climates, solar shading and good ventilation should be prioritised to keep spaces cool during the day. In colder climates, insulation and airtightness are key. Good cooling or heating systems are key in extreme environments. Thermal massing such as exposed stone, brick or concrete can be used in either warm or cold locations to help maintain comfortable temperatures.

Ensure a good supply of fresh air

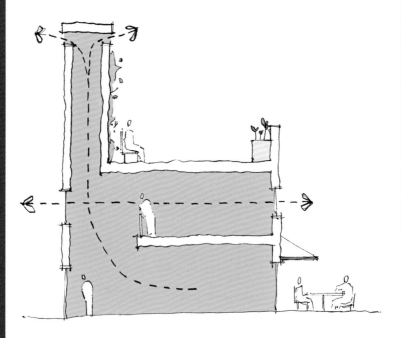

In a recent study, doubling ventilation rates reduced sick leave in staff by 35%

Over the last hundred years or so, a huge amount has been learned about the importance of clean, fresh air to our health. Chemicals such as nitrogen dioxide and larger particulate matter can cause us serious harm. Fresh air isn't just important for our physical health, however, but also for our mental wellbeing. By opening a window, we get a direct connection to the outside world, which is key given the amount of time we now spend indoors, as it boosts energy levels.

The sensation of a breeze against our skin is psychologically calming, and even a warm breeze will cool us, making us happier in hotter temperatures. Even better if it brings in the smells of flowers, grass, or rain on concrete, since these are also shown to be stress reducing.

Good natural ventilation can be provided through cross ventilation or stack ventilation, so this should be integrated where possible. This means designing buildings to be dual aspect (having two external facades), or to have some connection upwards to the sky. For cross ventilation to be effective, the distance across dual aspect spaces should be no more than four times their height. Where this can't be achieved, artificial ventilation is extremely important.

The benefits of natural ventilation need to be weighed against the quality of the air outside of the building, which can often be extremely poor in inner-city locations. While this can be improved through the use of plants or air filters, it is a factor to consider.

Keep the noise out

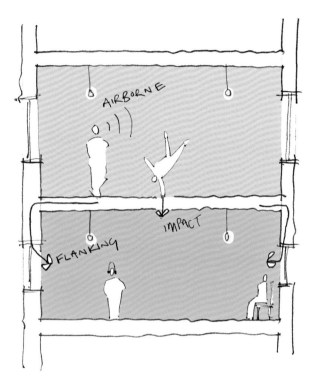

A noise reduction of 40dB means that loud speech outside can only just be heard – 50dB will mean that shouting can only be heard with great difficulty

If you stop for a moment right now and just see what you can hear, you may be surprised. There is a huge amount of background noise around us all the time, and we are usually completely oblivious to it. However, when it becomes intrusive it can severely impact our mental wellbeing, making us feel aggravated or even unsafe.

Many people report that noisy neighbours can trigger panic attacks or anxiety. It is therefore very important to acoustically insulate between flats and houses. Acoustic insulation should look to stop airborne sounds and impact noises and flanking noise. Soft furnishings, thick carpets and heavy curtains or drapes can also go a surprisingly long way to reducing the impact of noise, especially within a property itself. Existing buildings can also be retrofitted with under-carpet boards, new ceilings, window shutters or additional layers of board on walls to drastically improve acoustic performance.

Noise from roads or railways can severely disrupt sleep, which as previously discussed plays a key role in happiness (or lack of it). It can also impact on concentration and productivity in office environments. It is therefore important to make sure external walls, doors and windows provide good acoustic insulation. This can be problematic when combined with hot weather, as it is desirable to open windows to cool spaces, which unavoidably lets sound in. Other strategies such as solar shading or thermal massing (as previously discussed) can help mitigate this, but often artificial cooling is recommended in these situations.

3: CONTROL

The perception of control is closely linked to our happiness. Psychological studies have shown that if we believe we have more control we feel more content, even if our actual levels of control are unchanged. For example, a recent investigation into stress and commuting discovered that having little control over how you get to work can create a sense of 'impotence', which dramatically increases heart rates and the release of cortisol – a hormone related to stress.

A desire to regain control can be closely connected to many more long-term psychological problems such as eating disorders or obsessive behaviour.

When designing any building it is therefore paramount to ensure that its users feel like they have control over their immediate environment. As with most elements of design, simpler is better, and building users should always feel that it is straightforward for them to adjust a space to suit their specific needs.

Design adaptable spaces

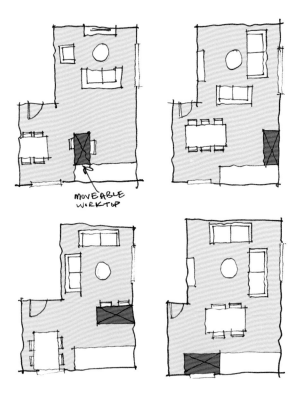

MOVEABLE
WORKTOP

By creating building elements that can be used in a variety of ways, designers can increase the control people have over how they use spaces

Over the last few decades, the sustainability movement has emphasised the importance of adaptable spaces, as this allows existing buildings to be reappropriated for alternative future uses.

However, giving current inhabitants the ability to adapt spaces to suit their needs has also been shown to make them feel happier and more empowered. This can mean allowing a living room to be arranged and used in a number of ways, or designing a workspace to allow furniture to slide away when not required, leaving an open, multi-purpose space.

This was prevalent in the work of Dutch structuralist architects such as Aldo van Eyck and Herman Hertzberger, who designed features such as stairs that could double up as seating. They argued that the designer's role is not to provide a complete solution but to allow users to take control of a building. By using the building in the ways they wanted, they would ultimately be happier within that space.

Give people better control over their environment

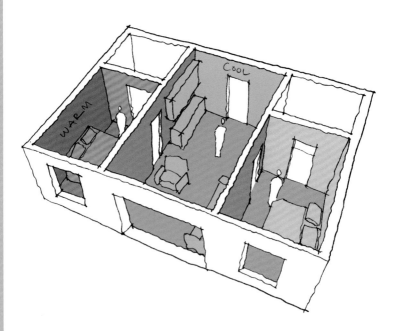

Having (or simply perceiving to have) more control over our environment has been shown to improve happiness

Given that people are shown to feel happier when they have more control, it is key that as designers, we give building users the tools to adapt their immediate environment. This can be as simple as giving employees the ability to open a window, or providing a dimmer switch rather than simply the choice of having the lights on or off.

Technology is now giving people even greater control over their environment. Apps and home hubs are now allowing people to adjust the lighting, music and temperature in their homes by voice or remotely, arguably making control simpler and more stress-free. Integration of these technologies should be considered at an early stage in the architectural design process, as should the capacity to accommodate more advanced systems as technology evolves further.

However, these systems should not render more traditional means of controlling our environment redundant. There is much to be said for the humble window shutter or a real log fire, and it could even be argued that we gain a greater sense of control and satisfaction from elements we can physically adjust ourselves.

Provide people with a range of environments

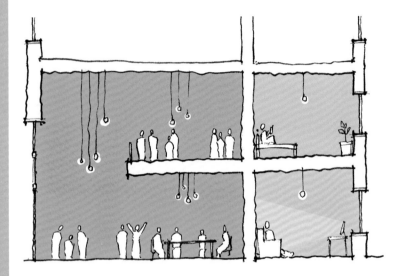

Experts estimate that between a third and a half of people are introverts, preferring environments that are not over-stimulating and relying on quiet time to re-energise

A good building should provide spaces for activity and spaces for calm. By creating spaces with varying characters, designers can give users direct control over the type of environment they choose to place themselves in.

For example, it is great for an office to contain large, busy, open-plan spaces where people can communicate easily and be highly sociable. However, a truly successful office will also include quieter retreat spaces where employees can escape the more chaotic side of their work and perhaps go to sketch, work on a written piece, take a phone call, or even just curl up with a book for a few minutes.

Allow for the personalisation of spaces

Employees who are allowed to personalise their space are up to 32% more productive

Following the modernist movement in the early 20th century, many architects and designers developed a passion for clean, minimal spaces. Photographs of interiors which appear almost uninhabited have been popular since architecture magazines were first published, and perhaps with good reason – the absence of distracting clutter brings attention to the form, light and materials.

However, the personalisation of spaces has been shown to be very important to our happiness. It is therefore important for designers to create spaces which allow for this personalisation. When people are restricted from making buildings or rooms their own, they lose an element of control and can even begin to resent a place. Ideally, give a building's inhabitants choice over (or at the very least some input into) colours, furniture or finishes where possible, and you will help to develop a sense of ownership and belonging.

Give people better control over their diets

A recent survey showed that millennials in the US spend around 44% of their food budget on eating out or takeaway food

What we eat can have a big impact on our mood and happiness. Humans have an incredibly complex relationship with food but, as a simple rule, eating a healthy and balanced diet will make us feel better physically and mentally. However, eating healthily takes more effort and is more expensive, so from time to time we all eat things that we know are worse for us.

For this reason, it is important to motivate people to spend time in their kitchens and cook more wholesome foods, rather than turning to convenient but unhealthy takeaway or processed alternatives. In homes, this means designing kitchens that are easy to use, and that are bright and pleasant to be in. The 'kitchen work triangle' is key to maximising usability. This refers to the relationship between the sink, hob and fridge, where the majority of cooking tasks take place. These three elements should therefore be located in close proximity to one another with clear routes between them. As the name suggests, placing them at the three points of a triangle rather than in a line is often cited as the most efficient relationship.

In many workplaces no kitchens are provided at all, making it harder for people to eat more healthily. Where possible designers should therefore aim to provide the best kitchens possible to give workers a broad choice in what they can cook and eat.

Give building users privacy

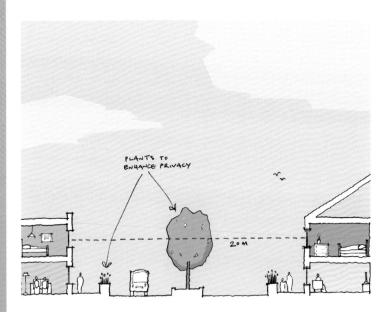

Privacy has been shown to support a sense of autonomy and individuality

Privacy is important to our mental wellbeing. It helps people to live life more freely and retain a sense of dignity, whereas a lack of privacy can feel restrictive and, for some, extremely upsetting. While it is particularly important in a residential setting, providing privacy has often been a relatively low priority for housebuilders, for whom density has traditionally taken precedent.

There are a number of rules to be followed here. Firstly, ensure that windows are a suitable distance away from facing neighbouring windows. Most UK guidance suggests around 20 metres as a suitable separation distance. It is also advisable to locate rooms so that similar functions face one another. For example, bedrooms should ideally face onto other bedrooms, not living spaces.

Privacy within the home itself is also important, and is an issue that has become more prevalent with the rise in popularity of open-plan living, which will be discussed in more depth later. While open-plan layouts are not a negative thing, subsidiary spaces should be provided to allow people privacy when required. This is one of the reasons that bedrooms are traditionally separated from the rest of the house, given the more private nature of their functions. Similarly, en-suite bathrooms should also be considered if possible, as they are another good way of improving privacy for members of the household.

4: NATURE

Spending time in nature has been shown unequivocally to improve our happiness and mental wellbeing, regardless of other factors. It has been proven to reduce stress, improve our memories, and make us kinder and more creative. It is almost impossible to overstate how good nature is for our minds.

However, with more than 50% of the world's population now living in cities and this figure set to rise, many of us are losing this vital connection with the outside world. This places a responsibility on designers to incorporate natural elements into buildings and the wider urban environment. The following section sets out a number of ways to approach this without breaking a project's budget or impacting deliverability.

Bring nature in

Biophilic design has been shown to reduce stress and increase the sense of being 'home'

Given that most people now spend more than 80% of their time inside, designers should look to create direct interaction with nature within buildings wherever possible. Plants offer a number of benefits to mood and happiness, as well as providing the emotional rewards associated with caring for and nurturing a living thing. They also clean the air we breathe, simultaneously improving our physical and psychological wellbeing.

Nature can be brought into buildings through something as simple as adding planters to a classroom, integrating an existing tree into a new building or creating an internal green wall, like my colleagues at Assael did in the atrium of their Great Western Quarter project, shown opposite. Species should always be selected carefully, ideally with the help of an arboriculturalist.

Provide views of nature

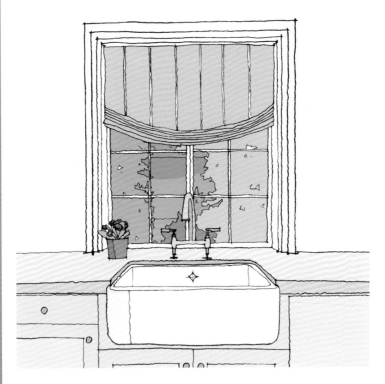

Research shows that regardless of other factors, 'nature relatedness' is a reliable predictor of happiness

While it is desirable to bring nature into buildings whenever we can, due to budget or build constraints it is not always possible to achieve this – at least not to the extent we would like.

In this situation, views of nature should be maximised. As humans, we seek out incredible views of mountains or oceans, even if it's only on our Instagram feeds. In fact, simply looking at nature has been shown to improve our mood. Coupled with the benefits to our eyes of spending a few minutes looking away from a screen, the value of good views even extends to preventing or relieving headaches.

While on most sites we are not able to give views of the Rocky Mountains or the Indian Ocean, in the majority of places it is possible to give people views of green space, water, or at least a tree. This should be capitalised upon wherever possible. If this is truly not achievable, investigate creative ways to introduce nature into the area surrounding your building – lobby your local council to plant a tree, buy your neighbour across the road some window boxes or, if you're feeling really brave, do some research into guerrilla gardening!

Put gardens on the roof

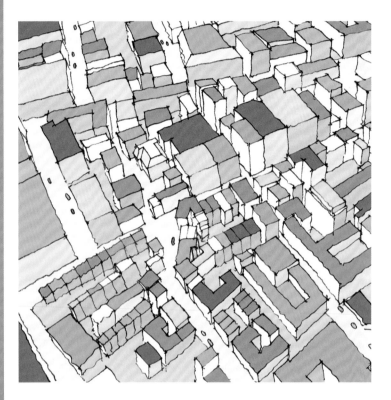

Roofscapes make up between 15 and 35% of the total land area of cities

Look at any aerial photo of a town or city and you'll see lots of disused space on the roofs of buildings. These roofs present a great opportunity for green space that would otherwise be wasted, and can often be a fantastic way to gain more garden space in dense urban situations. Although structure and waterproofing must be considered, new technologies are making rooftop gardens increasingly affordable and easy to construct.

Rooftop gardens actually have a number of benefits over their ground-level counterparts. Not only do they provide better views; they give us cleaner air and less noise than at street level. We also gain a feeling of taking refuge as we look down at the world from above, which is linked to a sense of safety and protection and can make us feel calmer.

Green roofs can improve the insulation of a building, reducing the need for heating and cooling, and can greatly improve biodiversity. Finally, rooftop gardens also offer benefits to neighbours with windows at higher levels, who get to look down on natural green blankets rather than concrete or felt roofing.

Design gardens and parks as an escape from the urban

People living in cities have been shown to have a more active amygdala, the part of the brain involved in assessing threats and generating fear

Living in an urban environment can be extremely stressful. It is therefore very important that city-dwellers are given opportunities to get a reprieve from this environment, if only for a short period of time.

Gardens and parks offer a fantastic opportunity to do this, and ideally should be designed in such a way that people feel like they are stepping out of the city. Central Park in New York is possibly the most famous example of this, but it is achievable on a smaller scale, as shown in London's Holland Park, or even in well-designed residential back gardens.

To achieve this effect, gardens and parks should firstly shield visitors from the city itself. Trees, planting or changes in level can be used to screen tall buildings, and also help with reducing the sound pollution from urban surroundings. This isn't to say that views of the city should not be provided from strategic locations, however, as these can create their own moments of joy.

Giving an outdoor space a more rural feel can also help, perhaps through the use of winding, unpaved paths that feel more like country tracks. Wildlife is also extremely important in helping to create a sense that we are out of the city, and is discussed later in this section.

Integrate or give views of water

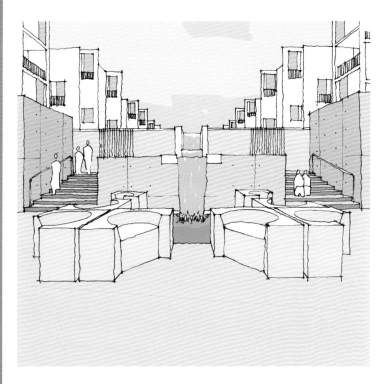

People who live near the ocean report having better mental wellbeing than those who don't

Given that water is a vital resource for humans, it is unsurprising that we find the presence of water calming. Villages were generally founded by initial settlers next to streams, rivers or seas thanks to the benefits they brought in terms of food, trade, and of course water itself. Studies have indeed shown that being near water makes us happier, so if it can be designed into projects it offers benefits that may make it worth the extra cost.

The challenge for architects and designers is how to integrate water into projects. Landscape design perhaps offers the best opportunity, as water can often be included in gardens in the form of ponds, streams or fountains, as at Louis Kahn's Salk Institute on the opposite page.

Inside buildings it can often be harder to design-in water, although there are many historical and vernacular examples of internal pools or fountains. If water features are to be used internally, however, they should be as simple as possible and require little maintenance. If there is no opportunity to bring water into a scheme, try to orient the building and its windows to give views of water.

Improve ecology and biodiversity

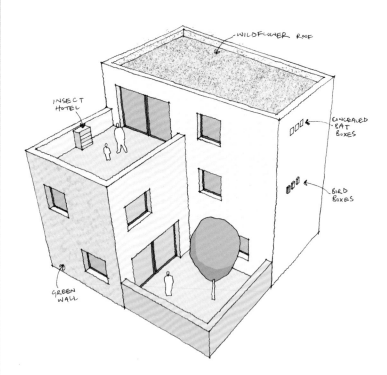

Interaction with animals and pets has been shown to help those suffering with depression

There are many reasons to increase the diversity of both animal and plant life on a construction project. The strongest argument for biodiversity is that it creates healthier and stronger ecosystems, which are extremely important for our planet to continue to function properly. However, having a rich ecosystem around us can also be highly beneficial to our mental wellbeing.

As previously discussed, increased plant life has been shown to make us happier and calmer. It can also offer physical benefits by reducing air pollution and offering cooling effects in high temperatures, making us more comfortable. A highly diverse range of plant life can result in bright, colourful displays, which can improve our mood.

Biodiverse plant environments can also attract wildlife, and interaction with animals has been shown to make most people happier. As discussed earlier, this can provide a psychological escape from the urban environment, help us to connect with nature, and help us to develop empathy. A variety of animal species are being forced out of urban locations, particularly those creatures which nest or roost in building fabrics, due to improvements in airtightness and construction techniques. A number of products are now available to provide homes for these species, including owls and peregrine falcons, without compromising a building envelope's quality or aesthetics.

Use nature to educate, engage and involve

A recent report by the RSPB concluded that four out of five children in the UK are not 'connected to nature'

If utilised in the right way, nature can be an effective way to improve people's happiness, co-ordination and self-confidence, and is now used extensively in rehabilitation and ecotherapy programmes. Activities such as group gardening have been shown to combat depression, improve self-esteem and energise people. Mental health charity Mind now recommends that ecotherapy be recognised as a clinically valid treatment for mental distress. This highlights the importance of gardens or a space to grow things within new developments, whether residential, commercial or educational.

Nature can be an effective educational tool. With the increase in urban living and screen-based activities, many children do not have a connection to nature, which could have damaging long-term effects on mental wellbeing. Designing-in educational features as shown on the previous page can be a fantastic way for children to learn about the world around them, as well as helping to improve ties to the natural world.

Finally, gardens can be a good way to help people feel included and empowered. The theory of participatory design argues that involving residents in the design process will increase their sense of ownership and pride in their buildings and surroundings. Studios such as the Edible Bus Stop have used this to great effect as part of community projects like Breaking Down Barriers, opposite. These successfully involve local residents in the design and construction of communal gardens.

5: AESTHETICS

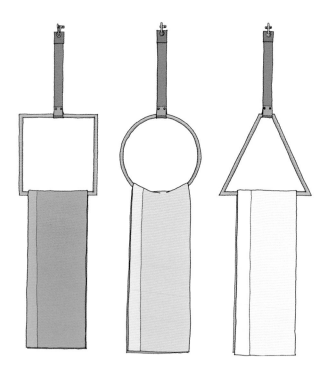

While this book has focused a great deal so far on how touch, sound and even smell can affect our mood, sight is undeniably one of our most important senses. Research into happiness in New York City, London, Paris, Toronto and Berlin has shown that visually attractive things and places make us unequivocally happier.

Therefore one of the biggest arguments for employing a good architect or landscape designer, buying furniture which looks (and of course feels) great, and filling your house with paintings you love is that it will make you a fundamentally happier person. The Danish, who spend the most money on furniture per capita of any country, believe that quality design influences our mood in a positive way, and that pleasant surroundings can help us to feel cosy and safe. The importance of aesthetics should not be underestimated.

It should be mentioned that taste inevitably makes it difficult to discuss visual elements of design. People have such widely varying opinions as to what is and is not attractive that designers must accept on some level that they will not please everybody. However, there are some rules that can be followed that will result in a visually more pleasant design: certain colours and proportions are generally more pleasing than others, for example. This section of the book explores some of the ways in which aesthetics can impact our happiness.

Use colour wisely (and sparingly)

In some studies the colour yellow has been shown to stimulate serotonin release in the brain

We have recently discovered that colour can have a greater effect on our disposition than previously realised. For example, blue streetlights are used in Tokyo, as it is believed they reduce crime and the rates of suicide by jumping in front of trains. Changing the colour of medicines has even been shown to influence their effectiveness, with red, orange and yellow best for stimulants, while blues and greens are better for tranquillisers.

Colour can be used to create a mood or an atmosphere at very little cost, and can even encourage socialising, evoke calmness or improve our focus. For example, yellow is a colour often associated with happiness and sunlight. It was used strikingly in the yellow flooring of Alvar Aalto's Paimio Sanatorium to emphasise brightness, as it reflected up onto ceilings and walls. Green and blue are generally considered more calming, and are better suited to bedrooms or quieter spaces. However, one of the reasons Aalto's use of colour was so successful was that it was confined to the flooring – too much colour can be overwhelming, so consider picking out details or individual walls in a colour rather than an entire space.

It should also be mentioned that colours have varying meanings and are interpreted in different ways from culture to culture. Red is often seen as a symbol of happiness and prosperity in Eastern cultures, while it can be associated with mourning in some African countries. It is therefore worth researching the cultural impact certain colours may have.

Create moments of joy

We generally let negative events affect our brains more than positive ones, so we must embrace and encourage moments of joy whenever possible

The design of many buildings nowadays is often heavily focused around regulations, cost-efficiency and buildability. While these are all key considerations, it is important not to forget that using these buildings must be a pleasurable experience.

In certain places in a building, designers should therefore look to create special moments that will perhaps bring a smile to somebody's face, or make them look twice at something they like. This could be a beautiful detail, a well-framed view, or an interesting use of materials such as the coloured glass in Le Corbusier's Notre Dame du Haut chapel, shown opposite. These moments do not have to be expensive, nor complex – in fact the cheaper and simpler they are, the more likely they are to make it through the value engineering and construction stages of a project as intended.

Avoid visual monotony

Research has shown that a lack of visual variety can lead to boredom, unhappiness and even higher mortality rates

Many of us walk around our towns and cities in a semi-daze, thinking about something that happened earlier that day or that we need to do later. Mindfulness teaches that we should instead try to engage in the present moment and focus on our surroundings. Research supports this theory, showing that too much daydreaming can actually make us unhappy.

It is therefore important that streets and buildings engage the people walking around them, both physically and visually. This can be achieved in many ways; for example, through more active facades featuring movement and pattern, such as in AHMM's Burntwood School on the opposite page. Materials can be used in an interesting way to catch the eye and bring us back to the present moment. This is not to say however that this should detract from a building's legibility, or make its function unclear, as will be discussed in the following section.

Internally, features such as shutters and tiles can add pattern to intrigue us, while prints and paintings can help to break up bland walls and create visual interest.

Make buildings and their parts legible

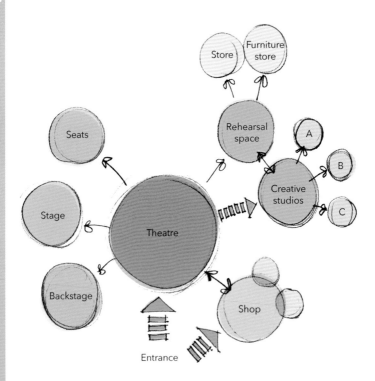

Buildings should be easy to understand. The EU Parliament building in Brussels is so confusing it is said to have made people cry!

While visual interest and aesthetic beauty are important, the legibility of streets, buildings and spaces also plays a large role in how pleasant we find places. Places should be straightforward to understand and use, so a balance needs to be struck between the beautiful and the practical.

Badly designed buildings can be confusing and frustrating, and ultimately make our experience of using them very unpleasant. This can affect our mood, particularly if we have to frequently use a building that is difficult to understand or navigate.

Legibility is important at all scales, from facades to bathroom taps. Buildings and their composite parts should be legible from a distance, on approach and during use. For example, the primary entrance to a building should always be simple to locate. As you get closer, it should become apparent which way the door opens, and you should get a sense of roughly how much force it is going to take to open it. Finally, the handle should be easily identifiable and clear in how it turns (or doesn't).

Celebrate the simple

Study participants tend to favour handmade items as gifts, often perceiving them to 'contain more love'

In much of the world now there is a 'culture of things'. We like to own things, and we especially like to buy new things. However, this obsession with material objects may not in fact be beneficial for our happiness, as we can never realistically satisfy that yearning for the next 'thing'.

The Japanese philosophy of *wabi sabi* is based around enjoying life as it happens, and shares ideas with traditional Zen Buddhism and what we now refer to as mindfulness. It argues that happiness is achieved internally, not externally, and that it can be gained from an appreciation of 'a beauty of things modest and humble', and your ability to be happy with what you have now.

These 'things' can be objects, such as a handmade bowl. *Wabi sabi* celebrates imperfection, which can make objects seem more 'human' and less manufactured, and support a sense of homeliness, helping us to feel safer and more at ease. This explains in part our tendency to prefer handmade over mass-produced items. When selecting construction materials or furnishings we should therefore consider whether they are *wabi sabi* or not: cheaper but more vernacular objects may in fact make us happier than their more expensive counterparts.

Wabi sabi can also refer to acts, such as making tea or showering. These moments can also be celebrated through design that focuses our attention on our actions. This is effectively a form of mindfulness, and has also been shown to improve mental wellbeing.

Get the proportions right

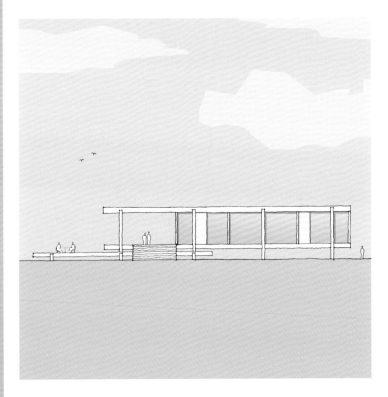

Mies van der Rohe would always draw proportions by eye, rather than basing dimensions on round units – the success of which can be seen in projects like Farnsworth House, above

When designing any physical object, its proportions are something we should consider at an early stage. At its simplest, an object's proportions are the ratio of its height to its width, and potentially also its depth. However, with more complex objects like a building or a car, we must also consider the relationships between one element and another; for example, the proportions of a window within a facade.

While it's difficult to say with certainty that particular proportions make us happier, some are definitely more pleasing to the eye. Many artists and architects, including da Vinci, Le Corbusier, Mondrian and Dalí, have experimented with the 'golden ratio' – where the length of an object is roughly one and a half times its width. It has been argued that these are the most aesthetically pleasing proportions since their discovery in 300BC by the mathematician Euclid.

It has also been argued that more common or easily recognised proportions are more satisfying to humans, as we find them comforting. This could also be the reason we find simple shapes such as squares or perfect circles pleasing.

6: ACTIVITY

We are all aware of the huge physical benefits of being active, but exercise also creates significant changes within our brains and can have an enormous impact on our mental wellbeing. Exercise releases hormones known as endorphins which activate the body's opiate receptors, improving our mood and reducing pain. Many authors have argued that the benefits of being active go even further than this, including giving us a clearer sense of identity and independence.

Unfortunately, however, most of us are fantastic at finding reasons to avoid exercise. This means we need it to be as easy as possible to be active, and designers can nudge us in the right direction through clever architecture or urban design. This chapter explains a variety of ways in which designers can gently encourage activity, with the ultimate goal of making people happier.

Encourage activity

Climbing stairs improves cardiovascular health and muscular development, and can burn more calories than jogging

Designers have a reasonable degree of control over how people use their buildings, even if a building's inhabitants are not directly aware of it. They should therefore try to encourage or persuade people to be active in the way they design buildings, as BVN Architecture did with their offices for Frasers Property, sketched on the opposite page.

An open, glassy, top-lit staircase, for example, might encourage people to walk up to the third floor rather than take the lift. Corridors should be generous and naturally lit to make movement around buildings a pleasant experience. Being active around the home or school can be made playful for both children and adults – some architects have experimented with rope ladders or climbing walls as ways for people to reach mezzanines or bunk beds, for example.

Design-in spaces for exercise

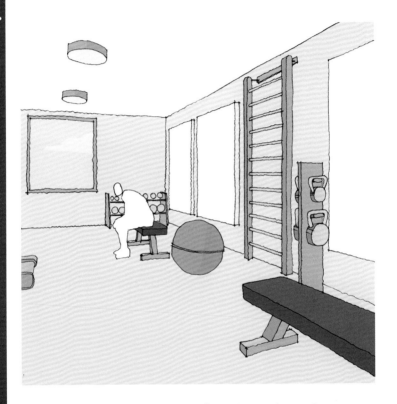

The mood benefits of 20 minutes of exercise can last 12 hours

As humans, we can all make excuses from time to time. Even the most motivated people will admit to occasionally finding a reason not to go for a run or to the gym. The most common excuses are not having time, or being too tired. This means that we need to make exercise as easy and as accessible for ourselves as possible, particularly when we are at our busiest or most tired.

Designers should therefore try to incorporate exercise facilities into buildings wherever possible. In-home or in-office facilities need not be high-tech or expensive: a pull-up bar and small cardio area with a few mats and a Swiss ball can be a great start. What matters is having a designated space that is free and ready whenever it is needed.

Shared public outdoor gym facilities have increased dramatically in popularity in recent years. These are great as they cost local councils very little to maintain and are free to members of the public, many of whom might not otherwise be able to gain access to expensive equipment. However, as set out above, they should be located where they are easy for people to access and use. Ideally, place them in the most concentrated areas of human activity to encourage maximum use.

Play areas are also of great importance. They encourage children to be active and engage with exercise at a young age. They also provide other key benefits, including brain development, improved social skills and production of Vitamin D when in daylight.

Design wider streets

Movement into our personal space activates the amygdala, the part of our brain that deals with threat and fear

The amount of personal space we are afforded can have a direct impact on our happiness. A lack of personal space has been shown to make people feel vulnerable, defensive and less happy. This is particularly important as we move from place to place.

Streets should therefore be designed with generous paths to allow pedestrians a comfortable amount of personal space. This is even more important when the level of activity or the speed of movement along a street is likely to be higher.

Designing wider streets also has the added bonus of allowing extra light into buildings on either side, which improves happiness and supports wellbeing. It can also be a way to integrate 'green links' through a city, connecting parks and green spaces and bringing nature into what are otherwise urban spaces.

Design for the bicycle

People with active lifestyles generally score higher in wellbeing analysis than those who are physically inactive

As well as being a good way to integrate exercise into our routine, regular cycling has been shown to positively affect happiness and help people to feel more relaxed. At a deeper level, it can increase self-esteem and nurture a sense of independence. As well as being a good way to integrate exercise into our routine, and reduce traffic and air pollution, regular cycling has been shown to positively affect happiness and help people to feel more relaxed.

Despite the fact that cycling reduces the risk of cancer and heart disease, bringing down the risk of early death by 41%, 'fear of being involved in a collision' was the highest reason people gave in a recent survey as to why they don't take up cycling. However, safe, well-designed cycle lanes and roads have been shown to encourage people to cycle to work, which can make it much easier for people to get daily exercise and the associated endorphin boost.

Secure and easy-to-use cycle parking has also been shown to increase people's willingness to commute in this way, and should be encouraged in all buildings, along with appropriate shower and changing facilities.

If possible, architects should also encourage clients and contractors to sign up to the CLOCS Standard for Construction Logistics, which aims to improve road safety in relation to construction vehicles and building sites.

Connect to nearby facilities

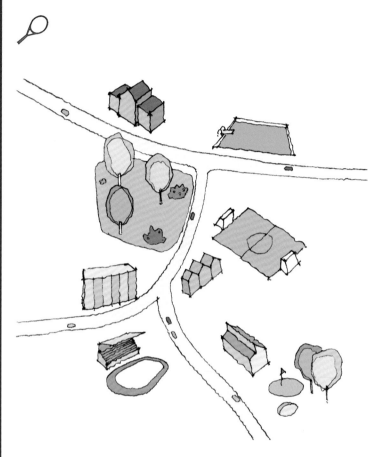

A recent 'free gym' scheme in Birmingham, UK, dramatically increased the uptake of exercise, particularly in women

Another important factor in how active people are is their access to sports facilities. In urban design, good connections to such facilities are of great importance.

In recent years there has been a significant reduction in amenities like sports centres, football pitches and tennis courts in many towns and cities, as urban densities have risen and land values have increased. It is important for authorities and developers to protect these facilities where at all possible, and to make them available to people from all social backgrounds.

New facilities should ideally be placed in well-connected locations to provide better access for all. This can mean being close to major roads or transport hubs, but can also mean being integrated directly into the centre of towns or cities.

Don't overlook spaces for inactivity

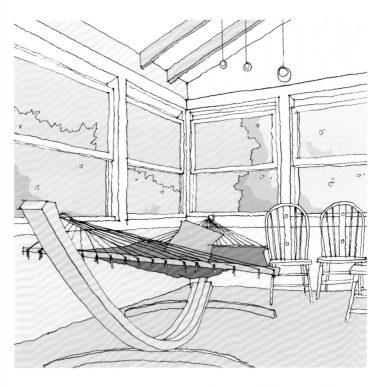

A phrontistery is the name for a place for quiet thinking or reflection

Rest is incredibly important for both body and mind. This doesn't necessarily mean sleeping, however. 'Quiet restfulness', which means sitting or lying awake but with our eyes closed, is also very beneficial.

Many buildings, however, provide no real 'quiet spaces'. Bedrooms are often used as a place of daytime retreat, despite not being designed primarily for this function. In offices these spaces almost never exist. Although it is sometimes difficult to convince clients of their importance, retreat spaces should be provided where possible as a way to allow people to take a short break from their hectic schedules.

These spaces should be designed to provide a true escape from the stresses of life. This means making them well acoustically insulated and dimly lit if possible. Furniture should be soft and inviting. Although a luxury, having a space specifically for napping or meditating can celebrate these acts that are highly nourishing for our minds.

7: PSYCHOLOGY

Every day, our moods are affected by things we may not even perceive. These can be things we have little control over, such as the weather or the way a person speaks to us. However, there are many aspects of daily life that impact our psychology which have been designed by other people, and these can affect us either positively or negatively.

We will often talk about the way a building makes us feel, but it can be quite difficult to understand exactly why it makes us feel that way. This section of the book examines some of the subtler aspects of design that have a big impact on our mood, despite most of us rarely thinking about them.

Don't overlook the importance of storage

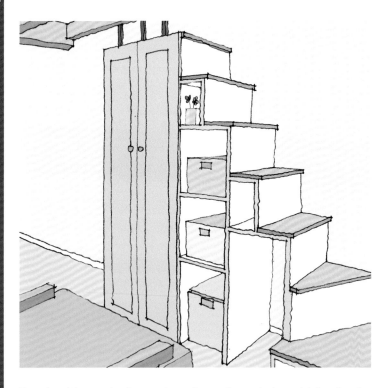

People with messier homes have been shown to have higher levels of the stress hormone cortisol

Research into the psychology of mess has now shown a direct link between untidiness and stress. We don't just find a tidy space more relaxing to be in; it is harder to concentrate when there is mess around. Perhaps then it is no coincidence that Scandinavian countries, which typically score very highly on happiness indexes, place a lot of value on storage in the home.

Modern developers tend to view storage as a low priority, as it takes up floor area that could be allocated to more economically valuable uses. Nooks and crannies, a common feature of older houses, are also disappearing as developers favour flat walls; however, these are traditionally where storage units such as bookshelves or wardrobes would be placed. This is leading to the frequent under-provision of storage, despite it being an important factor in how happy people feel in their homes. This also has an impact on how pleasant the external aesthetic is, as balconies become external storage areas for all kinds of objects.

It is therefore important that designers provide intelligent, integrated and generous storage. This can be concealed in other objects; for example, built into a staircase or below a bed. As a rule, drawer units are more efficient than shelves, so are often a better choice.

Provide high ceilings where possible

A link has been shown between high ceilings and a greater sense of psychological freedom

High ceilings are often sacrificed in buildings due to physical or financial constraints. However, they have been shown to create a sense of freedom and improve happiness, so they are worth fighting for in designs wherever possible.

If a high ceiling can't be achieved across a whole floor or building, try to provide them in special locations such as a double-height entry space to an office building, or a social space in a house. It is often worth sacrificing some upper floor area if there is the possibility to make the living space below more pleasant. As basement extensions have increased in popularity, many houses now feature double-height elements as a way to bring more light into lower ground spaces.

Celebrate the entrance

Home plays an important part of our self-definition, and can strongly affect our concept and view of ourselves

Despite its importance, the entrance to a building is often an under-considered design element. As the point of arrival, it creates the first impression of a building and sets the tone for the spaces beyond. It is also the only part of a building that everybody is guaranteed to use. An entrance therefore presents a good opportunity to influence how people perceive and experience a building.

A poor entrance may be one that is difficult to find or that makes a building seem uninviting. On the other hand, a successful entrance can create a sense of home or of a welcoming place that you would like to spend time in. An entrance does not need to be grand, but it should be clearly defined and have a strong sense of identity. This can be achieved through very small gestures, for example in subtle recesses to apartment doors in corridors, which give each entrance a sense of independence from the others.

Go open plan

Frequent contact with family and friends has been shown to substantially improve many common mental health problems

Open-plan living areas have been the subject of debate for some time. However, once all factors are taken into consideration, open-plan buildings offer many elements that can benefit happiness. Psychologically they can create a greater sense of space, which can make us feel happier and more relaxed.

An open-plan home also encourages us to be more social, which can prevent isolation. Connecting with family and friends on a more frequent basis is shown to benefit our mental wellbeing. However, as explained previously, private spaces should be provided elsewhere in the home or workplace to allow for escapism. Open-plan living also tends to offer the benefit of increased daylight, which as already discussed is important for our mental wellbeing.

However, open-plan buildings can create issues regarding noise and the aforementioned reduction in privacy for occupants. Perhaps an ideal solution therefore is to provide users with the ability to open or close off spaces as required, giving them increased control over their environment.

Bigger isn't always better

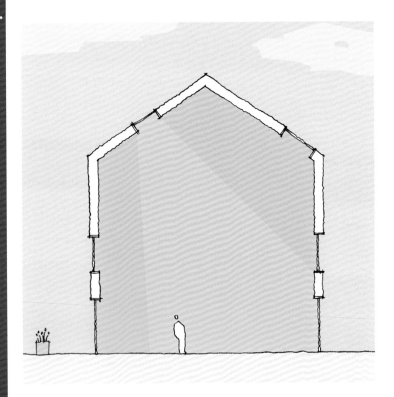

While often overlooked, the spatial qualities of buildings can have a dramatic impact on how we feel within them

Given the importance of personal space and privacy, there is certainly such a thing as too small a space. If a house, office or classroom is too small, it can be unpleasant and impact negatively on our mental wellbeing.

However, a number of theories suggest that having too much space can also be a negative thing. The Swedish principle of *lagom* is based around the idea of having 'just the right amount'. This is similar to the 'Goldilocks principle', where the aim is to provide a space that is neither too small nor too big, but instead is well-suited to its purpose.

Spaces that are oversized, whether internal or external, can leave people feeling dwarfed or isolated, which can have an unpleasant psychological impact. Bigger buildings can also be harder to maintain, resulting in unnecessary stress and potential anxiety. On the other hand, a smaller house will give you more free time, which can create a greater sense of freedom.

Finally, in a smaller building there is much less opportunity to hoard, and we are far more likely to keep only the possessions we really need. Reducing the quantity of material things we own has been reported by many people to improve their mental wellbeing, through drawing focus to what really makes them happy.

Consider prospect and refuge theory

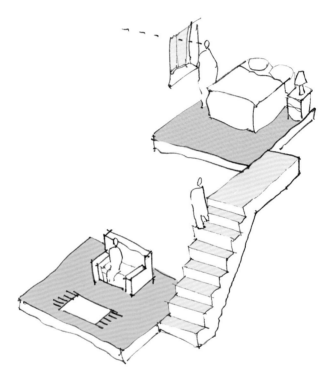

Lacking a feeling of safety can be a major trigger for a number of mental health issues

Jay Appleton's 1975 theory of 'prospect and refuge' argues that humans have evolved to feel innately safer in spaces that allow us to see without being seen. This underlines again the importance of privacy in determining our happiness.

As such, designers should stick to the tradition of first-floor bedrooms where possible, with living spaces below. The ascent to bed has become accepted design wisdom for a good reason: the elevation and outlook gives us a greater sense of safety and can help improve our sleep.

The importance of perceived safety goes beyond getting a good night's rest, however. Maslow's hierarchy of needs sets out safety as a basic requirement, surpassed only by physiological needs such as food, water and sleep. Without this feeling of safety, Maslow argued, people will feel anxious, tense and unhappy.

Create an atmosphere

Hygge has been referred to as 'the art of creating intimacy'

The atmosphere of a space is possibly the hardest element to pin down. What gives a pleasant atmosphere or 'feel' to a space is extremely subjective. However, a good atmosphere is particularly important for restaurant, retail and residential design.

Different parts of the world have their own rules for or approaches to creating successful atmospheres in spaces. For example, in Denmark people refer to *hygge*: an atmosphere of cosiness and intimacy achieved through warmth, soft furnishings and good lighting. In contrast, the Chinese philosophy of *feng shui* argues that a building will feel good if it is designed around balance and the flow of spaces. Contemporary Western design philosophy tends to be more closely connected to ideas of 'homeliness' and feeling relaxed within a space.

In reality, the right atmosphere for a space depends on many factors. However, creating the right feel for any place can be achieved by using many of the design ideas already discussed, such as lighting, colour, texture, furniture, and strong aesthetic design.

CONCLUSIONS

Our happiness, like most emotions, can be both subjective and quick to change. As such, designing for happiness will mean different things to different people.

However, in this book I have tried to provide a toolkit of ways in which you as a designer can support people's mental wellbeing through the buildings you create. These tools are summarised in an 'at-a-glance' list of key concepts below:

- Ensure both quality and quantity of light are provided, suitable for each space's purpose
- Consider touch and sound when designing, not just sight
- Make buildings comfortable spaces in which to spend time
- Give people good control over buildings and how they use them
- Design with the mindset that buildings should enable rather than inhibit their users
- Involve plants, water and wildlife wherever possible (and practical!)
- Help people forget occasionally that they are in cities
- Use the aesthetics of design to create visual interest and joy
- Make your designs easy to understand
- Encourage building users to be active

- Provide calm spaces for escape and relaxation
- Provide generous storage
- Make spaces open and airy, but designed for human scale
- Create a sense of home

It is also important to note that many clients, particularly in the commercial sector, may not be motivated by the idea of supporting their building users' mental wellbeing. In this case, however, there is always an argument to be made that these concepts add financial value to a project, for example through more productive office workers (in the UK, work-related stress, depression or anxiety accounted for 40% of work-related ill-health and 49% of working days lost in 2016/17), or tenants who will have fewer complaints in an apartment building. It is part of the role of designers to convince clients that these features are worth integrating.

On the following pages, I have explored how a model 'happy home' might look, incorporating some of the ideas set out in this book to create a nurturing environment for its inhabitants' mental wellbeing. I hope it inspires you to create your own happy designs.

1. Building oriented with key spaces to the south
2. Over 25° angle to any overshadowing
3. High-level bathroom window for light and privacy
4. Rooflights create drama above entrance
5. Warm, indirect light in living spaces
6. Tactile flooring used where possible
7. Tactile cladding encourages touch
8. Furniture selected for comfort and aesthetics
9. Windows arranged for cross and stack ventilation
10. Acoustically insulated walls and floors
11. Adaptable living spaces
12. Quiet meditation or reading space provided
13. Personalisation of rooms
14. Generous cooking and preparation spaces
15. 20m to neighbours' windows
16. Roof terrace creates calm urban amenity space
17. Framed views of nature
18. Gardens provided where site allows
19. Wildflower roof promotes biodiversity
20. Planters allow for urban gardening
21. Green wall to roof terrace
22. Colour used selectively to support mood
23. Timber battens minimise echoes and provide moment of joy upon entry
24. Well-proportioned, asymmetrical windows avoid visual monotony
25. Handmade or 'imperfect' quality to many building elements
26. Rooflight above stairs to celebrate activity
27. Bike hangers to encourage exercise
28. Built-in storage throughout home
29. Double-height space at entrance
30. Celebration of entrance with recess and use of colour
31. Open-plan ground floor to encourage social interaction
32. Spaces are generous, but not oversized
33. Bedrooms located on upper floor for increased sense of security

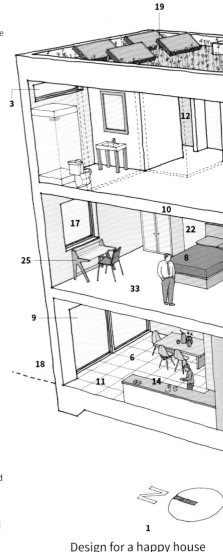

Design for a happy house

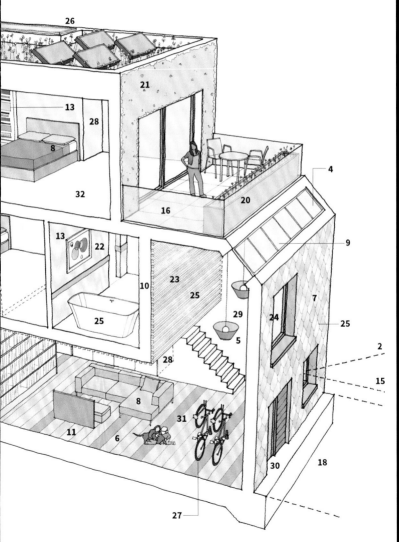

NOTES + REFERENCES

INTRODUCTION

Le Corbusier's *Vers une architecture* translates literally as 'Toward an Architecture' but is more commonly known as 'Towards a New Architecture' after the 1927 translation by Frederick Etchells of this name. It was one of the most influential architectural books of the 20th century, setting out Le Corbusier's theory of modern architecture [Le Corbusier, *Vers une architecture*, Editions G. Crès et Cie., Paris, 1923].

The World Health Organization reported that depression is now the leading cause of ill-health and disability worldwide in a news release on 30 March 2017 [A. Brunier and F. Chaib, '"Depression: let's talk" says WHO, as depression tops list of causes of ill health', World Health Organisation, <http://www.who.int/mediacentre/news/releases/2017/world-health-day/en/>, 2017 (accessed 12 February 2018)].

Many countries now run Mental Health First Aid courses, which aim to give people the practical skills to support mental health. I undertook my course through MHFA England, and would recommend it to anybody interested in learning more about mental health [Mental Health First Aid England, <https://mhfaengland.org>, 2018 (accessed 12 February 2018)].

A number of studies have shown that mindfulness or meditation can reduce the size of parts of the brain related to stress and anxiety [A.A. Taren, J.D. Creswell, P.K. Gianaros, 'Dispositional Mindfulness Co-Varies with Smaller Amygdala and Caudate Volumes in Community Adults', *PLoS ONE*, 8(5): e64574, <http://journals.plos.org/plosone/article?id=10.1371/journal.pone.0064574>, 2013 (accessed 23 April 2018)].

LIGHT

The *WELL Building Standard* (a design standard promoting health and wellness in occupants of buildings) supports the idea that psychological health is benefited by exposure to natural light, and has a section devoted to light. This provides more detailed advice on designing with natural and artificial light in mind [Delos Living LLC, *WELL Building Standard Version 1.0*, New York, 2014].

Some of the most compelling evidence regarding the impact of light on our wellbeing and sleep health can be found in a study published in the *Journal of Clinical Sleep Medicine*, including the fact that staff get 46 minutes less sleep a night if they have no windows [M. Boubekri, I. Cheung, K. Reid, C.H. Wang and P. Zee, 'Impact of windows and daylight exposure on overall health and sleep quality of office workers: a case-control pilot study', *Journal of Clinical Sleep Medicine*, 10(6), <https://www.ncbi.nlm.nih.gov>, 2014 (accessed 12 February 2018)]. I must thank Phil Hampshire from BuroHappold for pointing me towards this study in their fantastic 2017 presentation 'Winning in the Workplace' [A. Keelin, D. Price and P. Hampshire, 'Winning in the Workplace', *BuroHappold Engineering*, <https://www.burohappold.com/wp-content/uploads/2017/03/Creating-a-winning-workplace.pdf>, 2017 (accessed 12 February 2018)].

For more information about how light affects us physically, see Christopher Bergland's comprehensive article on the subject [C. Bergland 'Exposure to Natural Light Improves Workplace Performance', *Psychology Today*, <https://www.psychologytoday.com/blog/the-athletes-way/201306/exposure-natural-light-improves-workplace-performance>, 2013 (accessed 12 February 2018)].

Orient buildings sensitively

Selecting where and how to place a building on site is one of
the most important decisions in the entire design process, as it
will impact many of the decisions that follow. *The Environments
of Architecture: Environmental Design in Context* provides a good
overview of the environmental considerations involved in such a
decision, including daylight, in its second chapter 'Site and setting'
[R. Thomas and T. Garnham 'Site and setting' in *The Environments
of Architecture: Environmental Design in Context*, Taylor & Francis,
Abingdon, 2007].

The website for *Green Passive Solar Magazine* also offers good
advice on building orientation and seasonal considerations in
relation to solar gains [*Green Passive Solar Magazine*, <https://
greenpassivesolar.com> (accessed 12 February 2018)].

Consider shadows

When considering overshadowing (and in fact many other
environmental considerations), Sofie Pelsmakers' *The Environmental
Design Pocketbook* is a great place to start, containing detailed design
advice and useful diagrams [S. Pelsmakers, *The Environmental Design
Pocketbook*, RIBA Publishing, London, 2012].

In the UK at least, local authority advice can also be very helpful.
While design advice varies from one authority to the next, an angle
of around 25° and a distance of around 18–20m to nearby properties
is typical.

Be selective about window sizes

While it is good practice to appoint an environmental consultant to
review daylight levels on larger projects, architects and designers
can find good guidance in a research paper entitled 'Daylight
Design Rules of Thumb', which is available online. This offers

advice on elements such as window area:floor area and room depth [N.L. Ibrahim and S. Hayman, 'Daylight Design Rules of Thumb', *Conference on Sustainable Building South East Asia*, <https://www.irbnet.de/daten/iconda/CIB_DC23487.pdf>, 2005 (accessed 12 February 2018)].

Christopher Alexander's classic *A Pattern Language: Towns, Buildings, Construction* also provides an interesting discourse on specifying window sizes. Alexander supports the idea that window sizes should be individually considered, arguing: 'on no account use standard doors or windows. Make each window a different size, according to its place' [C. Alexander, S. Ishikawa, & M. Silverstein, *A Pattern Language: Towns, Buildings, Construction*, Oxford University Press, New York, 1977, p. 1048].

Avoid deep plans

As mentioned above, 'Daylight Design Rules of Thumb' provides good information on room depth, citing a number of sources which generally agree that room depth should be around twice the height of its windows for comfortable natural daylighting.

The *WELL Building Standard* also recommends that the 'lease depth' (distance between the core and facade) for offices does not exceed 7.5m for 75% of the area for all regularly occupied spaces. Smaller distances should be considered for residential buildings, where windows are generally smaller and ceilings lower [Delos Living LLC, *WELL Building Standard Version 1.0*, New York, 2014].

Use high-level windows to combine light and privacy

The case for the importance of privacy to mental wellbeing has been made numerous times, but perhaps most convincingly in Carl D. Schnieder's *Shame, Exposure and Privacy*, where he defends humanity's basic need for privacy and for places in which to be vulnerable. When it is not desirable to allow direct views into a space, designers should still look to provide natural light and a connection to the outside world, and high-level windows can be an effective way to achieve this [C. Schneider, *Shame, Exposure and Privacy*, Beacon Press, Boston, 1977].

Use rooflights shrewdly

As explained in the main body of this book, a rooflight should not be viewed as a substitute for a window. However, they do have their merits, and can transform a space when used in addition to traditional windows.

Although clearly not an unbiased source, the National Association of Rooflight Manufacturers (NARM)'s 2015 technical document 'NTD12' puts forward many sound arguments for the value of rooflights. It is also a great source of information on different types of daylight, daylight quality and daylight factor [NARM Secretariat, 'An introduction to natural daylight design in domestic properties', NARM, <http://www.narm.org.uk/uploads/pdfs/NARM_NTD12. pdf>, 2015 (accessed 15th February 2018)].

Don't overlook artificial light

The research showing that bright lights can create more intense emotions was taken from a study carried out at the University of Toronto Scarborough called 'Incandescent affect: Turning on the hot emotional system with bright light'. It showed that depression-prone people can become more depressed under brighter lights, referring to the fact that suicide rates peak during the sunnier months of late spring and summer [A. Jing Xu and A. Labroo, 'Incandescent affect: Turning on the hot emotional system with bright light', *Journal of Consumer Psychology*, 24(2):207–

216, <https://www.sciencedirect.com/science/article/pii/
S1057740813001174>, 2014 (accessed 15 February 2018)].

Whether specifying lighting for a project or selecting lamps
for your own home, the *WELL Building Standard* provides useful
information on glare control for artificial lighting [Delos Living
LLC, *WELL Building Standard Version 1.0*, New York, 2014, p. 95].

For further depth, Hervé Descottes, and Cecilia E. Ramos'
Architectural Lighting: Designing with Light and Space offers design
advice and more detailed technical information on artificial light
design [H. Descottes and C. Ramos, *Architectural Lighting:
Designing with Light and Space*, Princeton Architectural Press, New
York, 2011].

Consider the temperature of artificial light

One of the most informative studies on the impact of artificial
light temperatures on people is a 1996 Japanese study which
demonstrated that higher (cooler) light temperatures suppressed
the nocturnal drop in core temperature and nocturnal melatonin
release generally associated with sleep [T. Morita and H. Tokura,
'Effects of lights of different colour temperature on the nocturnal
changes in core temperature and melatonin in humans', *Housing
Science Division, Comprehensive Housing R&D Institute*,
<https://www.ncbi.nlm.nih.gov/pubmed/8979406>, 1996
(accessed 15 February 2018)].

Again, Descottes, and Ramos' *Architectural Lighting* is a great
source of information, which covers the physics behind the colour
of light, and why different types of artificial lighting provide
different temperatures and qualities [H. Descottes and C. Ramos,
Architectural Lighting: Designing with Light and Space, Princeton
Architectural Press, New York, 2011].

Use artificial light to create pockets of calm

In recent years the phrase 'self-care' has become increasingly popular in the media as society has gained a greater appreciation of the importance of looking after ourselves and our own wellbeing. Sherrie Bourg Carter's *Psychology Today* article is one such piece that highlights the importance of quiet escapism [S. Bourg Carter, '6 Reasons You Should Spend More Time Alone', *Psychology Today*, <https://www.psychologytoday.com/blog/high-octane-women/201201/6-reasons-you-should-spend-more-time-alone>, 2012 (accessed 15 February 2018)]. There are many more out there, including a piece I wrote on this subject for *ArchDaily*, albeit more focused on architects themselves [B. Channon, 'Why Architects Should Start Being a Little More Selfish', *ArchDaily*, <https://www.archdaily.com/888807/why-architects-should-start-being-a-little-more-selfish>, 2018 (accessed 15 February 2018)].

When considering ways to create private pockets of calm in the home, Rebecca Weir's and Allyson Coates' *The Languages of Light* provides design inspiration, case studies and practical considerations for residential lighting [R. Weir and A. Coates, *The Languages of Light*, Artifice Books on Architecture, London, 2015].

COMFORT

The *WELL Building Standard* also argues the importance of comfort in wellbeing, and offers useful advice on topics including ergonomics, noise and thermal comfort [Delos Living LLC, *WELL Building Standard Version 1.0*, New York, 2014].

The BCO standards are also a good reference for the design of offices, providing further guidance on temperature and acoustics [BCO 'Best Practice Guides', *British Council for Offices*, <http://www.bco.org.uk/Research/Best-Practice-Guides.aspx>, 2017 (accessed 15 February 2018)].

If you are interested in reading more about how a mindful approach can impact our happiness, there are now a huge number of books on this subject. However, I would personally recommend Rob Nairn's *Diamond Mind: A Psychology of Meditation*, which gives a thorough insight into how mindfulness can affect the way we see the world [R. Nairn, *Diamond Mind: A Psychology of Meditation*, Shambala Publications, Inc., Boston, 1999].

Use tactile materials

The typical architectural approach is one that prioritises the sense of sight above all others. However, a different philosophy is presented in Juhani Pallasmaa's *The Eyes of the Skin*, which questions why the visual sense has 'become so predominant in architectural culture and design'. This extremely evocative book suggests a range of ways in which buildings can engage the other senses and is a must-read for anybody looking to create buildings that we engage with at a more physical level [J. Pallasmaa, *The Eyes of the Skin*, John Wiley & Sons Ltd., Chichester, 2012].

David J. Linden's *Touch: The Science of Hand, Heart and Mind* is effectively a thesis on the importance of this sense, and argues that it is generally overlooked. While not architecture-related, it is an interesting read for those who would like to know more about how touch affects us in ways we often don't realise [D. Linden, *Touch: The Science of Hand, Heart and Mind*, Viking, New York, 2015].

Consider comfort as well as aesthetics

When selecting furniture, there is no real substitute for physically testing each piece in person, and this should be encouraged wherever possible. For a comprehensive written introduction to furniture design, however, it is difficult to look past Stuart Lawson's *Furniture Design: An Introduction to Development, Materials* and Manufacturing [S. Lawson, *Furniture Design: An Introduction to Development, Materials and Manufacturing*, Laurence King Publishing Ltd., London, 2013].

For further information and advice on sleep, the Mental Health Foundation's website is a very good place to start ['Your Mental Health', *Mental Health Foundation*, <https://www.mentalhealth.org.uk/your-mental-health>, 2018 (accessed 15 February 2018)].

Think about the temperature of buildings

As with lighting, it is prudent to appoint a specialist environmental consultant to assess issues such as overheating on larger design projects, but there are good guides and rules of thumb that can be integrated into designs at an early stage.

101 Rules of Thumb for Low Energy Architecture by Huw Heywood provides useful advice and diagrams about how buildings can naturally maintain comfortable temperatures through well-considered design [H. Heywood, *101 Rules of Thumb for Low Energy Architecture*, RIBA Publishing, London, 2013], as does the previously mentioned *The Environments of Architecture* [R. Thomas and T. Garnham, *The Environments of Architecture: Environmental Design in Context*, Taylor & Francis, Abingdon, 2007].

Beyond this, minimum insulation levels (U-values) and airtightness values are likely to be set out in the building regulations, depending where in the world the project is. In recent years these have become more demanding, and it seems likely that much of the focus in coming years will be on finding ways to naturally cool buildings.

Ensure a good supply of fresh air

As well as guidance on natural light, Sofie Pelsmakers' *The Environmental Design Pocketbook* also provides useful information on how to naturally ventilate buildings [S. Pelsmakers *The Environmental Design Pocketbook*, RIBA Publishing, London, 2012]. In simple terms the advice is: avoid single-aspect spaces if you can, and use cross or stack ventilation wherever possible.

BREEAM (an international scheme that certifies the sustainability performance of buildings) provides guidance on how to achieve good indoor air quality ['BREEAM Knowledge Base', *BREEAM*, <https://kb.breeam.com/> (accessed 15 February 2018)], while the UK's Building Regulations (slightly contradictorily) provide minimum standards on both the ventilation and airtightness of buildings ['Ventilation: Approved Document F', *RIBA Online Bookshop*, <https://www.gov.uk/government/publications/ventilation-approved-document-f>, 2010 (accessed 15 February 2018)].

Keep the noise out

Noise pollution has also been in the headlines recently, with the World Health Organization describing the 'burden of disease from environmental noise' in a thorough report on the subject [WHO Regional Office for Europe, 'Burden of disease from environmental noise – Quantification of healthy life years lost in Europe', World Health Organization, <http://www.who.int/quantifying_ehimpacts/publications/e94888/en/>, 2017 (accessed 15 February 2018)]. Acousticians are often called in to ensure noise levels are acceptable on major projects, but if this is not the case, the UK Building Regulations provide advice and details which can be applied to achieve acceptable acoustic separation ['Resistance to sound: Approved Document E', *RIBA Online Bookshop*, <https://www.gov.uk/government/publications/resistance-to-sound-approved-document-e>, 2015 (accessed 15 February 2018)]. While this is a British regulatory document, the advice could be useful for projects worldwide.

Chapter X of Steen Eiler Rasmussen's *Experiencing Architecture* provides an interesting discussion on the acoustics of buildings, although less technical and more theoretical [S.E. Rasmussen, 'Hearing Architecture' in *Experiencing Architecture*, The MIT Press, Cambridge, Massachusetts, 1959].

CONTROL

The study into stress and commuting referenced in this chapter was carried out in 2004 by Dr David Lewis [A. Clark, 'Want to feel less stress? Become a fighter pilot, not a commuter', *The Guardian*, <https://www.theguardian.com/uk/2004/nov/30/research.transport>, 2004 (accessed 15 February 2018)].

In his *New York Times* best-selling book Delivering Happiness, Tony Hsieh argues that 'happiness is really just about four things: perceived control, perceived progress, connectedness, and vision/meaning (being part of something bigger than yourself)' [T. Hsieh, *Delivering Happiness: A Path to Profits, Passion and Purpose*, Business Plus, New York, 2010].

This idea that perceived control affects our happiness has been demonstrated in a number of studies, including 'Is Feeling "in Control" Related to Happiness in Daily Life?', which confirms that a generalised sense of control is important to wellbeing [R. Larson, 'Is Feeling "in Control" Related to Happiness in Daily Life?', *Psychological Reports*, 64:775-784 <http://journals.sagepub.com/doi/abs/10.2466/pr0.1989.64.3.775>, 1989 (accessed 15 February 2018)].

While a truly 'mindful' approach would be to acknowledge the lack of control in day-to-day life and accept it for what it is, this is difficult for even the most experienced of mindfulness coaches. A more sympathetic approach is to make the argument that, if a greater perception of control tends to make people happier, we should strive to provide that sense of control in buildings wherever possible.

Design adaptable spaces

The *WELL Building Standard* also touches on adaptable spaces, arguing that spaces should be 'sufficiently adaptable for working, focusing, collaborating and resting as needed'. This can be seen in many of the case-study projects on their website ['WELL Projects', International WELL Building Institute, <https://wellonline. wellcertified.com/community/projects>, 2017 (accessed 15 February 2018)].

To learn more about the true masters of adaptable spaces, however, I would refer you to the works of structuralists Herman Hertzberger and Aldo Van Eyck. Hertzberger's *Lessons for Students in Architecture* [H. Hertzberger, *Lessons for Students in Architecture*, nai010 Publishers, Rotterdam, 2009] and Robert McCarter's *Aldo Van Eyck* [R. McCarter. *Aldo van Eyck*. Yale University Press, New Haven, 2015] both contain case studies (in the form of photographs and drawings) of these two great architects' work.

Give people better control over their environment

With the current rate of technological advancement for home and office environmental control systems, any books or products I reference here will likely be outdated before this book goes to press. However, a few simple rules apply and seem likely not to change with the advance of technology: choose systems that are easy to use for people of all ages and abilities, ensure systems result in a net time-saving, and make sure that any means of control are empowering and not restrictive.

Provide people with a range of environments

Susan Cain's 2012 book *Quiet: The Power of Introverts in a World That Can't Stop Talking* reports that between 33% and 50% of the

American population are 'introverts', and is an interesting study into how introverts and extroverts differ [S. Cain, *Quiet: The Power of Introverts in a World That Can't Stop Talking*, Penguin, London, 2012]. A number of reports, such as 'Extraversion and Happiness', conclude that extroverts are often found to have higher levels of happiness than introverts, which provides a further reason to provide quieter spaces for introverts to experience a moment's calm [W. Pavot, E. Diener and F. Fujita. 'Extraversion and Happiness', *Personality and Individual Differences*, 11(12):1299-1306, <https://www.sciencedirect.com/science/article/pii/019188699090157M>, 1990 (accessed 17 February 2018)].

Allow for the personalisation of spaces

Personalisation is a way to increase our sense of ownership and our emotional connection with a space.

A study by Dr Craig Knight of Exeter University's School of Psychology investigated this phenomenon in office spaces. Its results consistently showed that the more control people had over their workplace, the happier and more motivated they felt. It seems reasonable to infer from this that increased control over other building types would have a similar impact [C. Knight, 'Designing your own workspace improves health, happiness and productivity', University of Exeter, <http://www.exeter.ac.uk/news/featurednews/title_98638_en.html>, 2010 (accessed 17 February 2018)].

Give people better control over their diets

A well-designed kitchen will be tailored to you or your client's personal needs and how they would like to use it. However, good rules of thumb for designing a user-friendly kitchen are available. Although given in inches, the (American) National Kitchen and Bath Association (NKBA)'s guidelines on kitchen design are extremely useful, and easy to find online. They also provide further information on the kitchen work triangle including sample layouts ['Thirty-One Ways to a Better Kitchen', Kitchens.com, <http://www.kitchens.com/design/layouts/nkba-guidelines/nkba-guidelines>, 2014 (accessed 17 February 2018)].

For those without CAD available to them, the NKBA also has an online 'Virtual Planning Tool', which allows non-professionals to design their own kitchens to a high level of customisation. It gives the ability to specify products and finishes, change the kitchen layout and dimensions, and add windows and services. Your designs can then be viewed in 3D, plan or elevation ['NKBA Virtual Planning Tool', NKBA, <http://nkba.2020.net/planner/UI/Pages/VPUI.htm>, (accessed 17 February 2018)].

Give building users privacy

Privacy in the built environment is an interesting topic, given that – as discussed within this book – social interaction is also an important part of society to support mental health. This is touched upon by Jane Jacobs in *The Death and Life of Great American Cities*, where she discusses the importance of the balance between public and private life [J. Jacobs, *The Death and Life of Great American Citie*,. Random House Inc., New York, 1993]. However, Jacobs acknowledges the undeniable human need for privacy (as already mentioned – Schneider's *Shame, Exposure and Privacy*).

The *WELL Building Standard* also recognises the role privacy plays in buildings, and provides guidance on designing spaces to 'unwind, focus and meditate' [Delos Living LLC, *WELL Building Standard Version 1.0*, New York, 2014, p. 139].

For those interested in a more academic discussion of this subject, Michael Georgiou's essay 'Architectural Privacy: A Topological Approach to Relational Design Problems' provides a thorough and

fascinating investigation into privacy and architecture
[M. Georgiou, 'Architectural Privacy: A Topological Approach to
Relational Design Problems', *Bartlett School of Graduate Studies*,
<http://discovery.ucl.ac.uk/2919/1/2919.pdf>, 2006 (accessed 17
February 2018)].

NATURE

The idea that humans possess an innate desire to be connected
to nature, although not entirely new, was popularised by Edward
O. Wilson's *Biophilia* in 1984, where he first introduced his
'biophilia hypothesis' [E.O. Wilson, *Biophilia*, Harvard University
Press, Cambridge, Massachusetts, 1984]. The term biophilia,
meaning 'love of life or living systems', was first used by German
psychologist and philosopher Erich Fromm in 1964 [E. Fromm, *The
Heart of Man: Its Genius for Good and Evil*, Harper & Row, New York,
1964]. Since then, a multitude of studies have supported Fromm's
and Wilson's theories, demonstrating that nature makes us happier
and reduces stress, on top of the many other benefits discussed in
this book.

Other good books on this subject include Clemens G. Arvay's *The
Biophilia Effect* [C. Arvay, *The Biophilia Effect: A Scientific and Spiritual
Exploration of the Healing Bond Between Humans and Nature*, *Sounds
True Inc.*, Louisville, 2018] and Florence Williams' *The Nature Fix*
[F. Williams, *The Nature Fix: Why Nature Makes Us Happier, Healthier,
and More Creative*. W. W. Norton & Company, New York, 2017].

Bring nature in

There are thousands of amazing built examples of how nature can
be incorporated into buildings. Philip Jodidio's book *Architecture:
Nature* contains numerous projects that, as the name suggests,
explore the relationship between architecture and nature, and

provides a good source of inspiration for anyone interested in how the two can complement each other [P. Jodidio, *Architecture: Nature*, Prestel, New York, 2006].

Two of the best architects working intimately with nature today are Stefano Boeri, famous for the Bosco Verticale (Vertical Forest) in Milan, and Vo Trong Nghia, a Vietnamese architect who seems to view plants as their own, very important material in his architectural palette. It is also worth mentioning that Nghia is a keen advocate of meditation, and recently paid for all 80 of his staff to attend a week-long retreat.

Provide views of nature

A number of studies have been carried out into how 'nature connectedness' affects our happiness, including 'Happiness and Feeling Connected' and 'Happiness is in our Nature', both by John M. Zelenski and Elizabeth K. Nisbet [J.M. Zelenski and K.E. Nisbet, 'Happiness and Feeling Connected', *Environment and Behaviour*, 46(1):3-23, <http://journals.sagepub.com/doi/abs/10.1177/0013916512451901>, 2012 (accessed 17 February 2018); and J.M.Zelenski and K.E. Nisbet, 'Happiness Is in Our Nature: Exploring Nature Relatedness as a Contributor to Subjective Well-Being', *Journal of Happiness Studies*, 12(2):303-322, <https://www.researchgate.net/publication/226840838_Happiness_Is_in_Our_Nature_Exploring_Nature_Relatedness_as_a_Contributor_to_Subjective_Well-Being>, 2011 (accessed 17 February 2018)].

This reinforces Christopher Alexander's argument that windows should be sized and placed to give both the right amount of light in and the best views out, ideally of nature. BREEAM guidance supports this, requiring that all positions within relevant building areas are within 7m of views out ['BREEAM UK New Construction', BRE Global Ltd., <https://tools.breeam.com/filelibrary/BREEAM%20

UK%20NC%202014%20Resources/SD5076_DRAFT_BREEAM_UK_
New_Construction_2014_Technical_Manual_ISSUE_0.1.pdf>,
(accessed 17 February 2018)].

If you are interested in increasing the amount of greenery in your
urban neighbourhood, guerrillagardening.org is the inspiring
(and often entertaining) website of the London-based Guerrilla
Gardening community, and is full of great ideas about how you
can 'gently encourage' horticulture where it may not currently
exist [Guerrilla Gardening.org, *Guerilla Gardening*, <http://www.
guerrillagardening.org> (accessed 17 February 2018)].

Put gardens on the roof

The statistic about how much of our cities' footprints are roofscapes
is from Stephen Peck of non-profit group Green Roofs for Healthy
Cities ['Urban Roofscapes: Using "Wasted" Rooftop Real Estate
to an Ecological Advantage', *Scientific American*, <https://www.
scientificamerican.com/article/urban-roofscapes-ecofriendly-
rooftops>, 2012 (accessed 17 February 2018)]. Their website is a great
source of further information on roof gardens and green roofs and
contains a very useful references section.

Roof gardens need not be large, but if they are they can almost be
designed using similar strategies to traditional gardens/landscaping
(notwithstanding considerations about roof build-up and structure).
If you are interested in ways to make a small, 'wasted' space into
a garden, Kay Maguire's and Tony Woods' *Big Ideas, Small Spaces*
[K. Maguire and T. Wood, *Big Ideas, Small Spaces*, Mitchell Beazley,
London, 2017] and Andrew Wilson's *Small Garden Handbook*
[A. Wilson, *RHS Small Garden Handbook: Making the most of your
outdoor space*, Mitchell Beazley, London, 2013] are beautiful guides to
turning under-appreciated areas (such as balconies and roofs) into a
green paradise.

Design gardens and parks as an escape from the urban

As we move towards a more urban society, designing suitable escapes from the city will become increasingly important. The aforementioned *The Environments of Architecture* [R. Thomas and T. Garnham, *The Environments of Architecture: Environmental Design in Context*, Taylor & Francis, Abingdon, 2007] estimates that, 'by mid-century we may be nine billion people with 70 per cent living in cities', resulting in around 6.3 billion urban dwellers.

Gayle Souter-Brown's *Landscape and Urban Design For Health and Well-Being* [G. Souter-Brown, *Landscape and Urban Design for Health and Well-Being: Using Healing, Sensory and Therapeutic Gardens*, Routledge, Abingdon, 2015] provides useful advice for designing parks and gardens that can re-invigorate us and support good mental wellbeing, as does *Therapeutic Gardens: Design for Healing Spaces* by Daniel Winterbottom and Amy Wagenfeld [D. Winterbottom and A. Wagenfeld, *Therapeutic Gardens: Design for Healing Spaces*, Timber Press, Portland, 2015].

The highly enjoyable *My Garden is a Car Park: and Other Design Dilemmas* by Kendra Wilson provides solutions to a number of common garden and landscape problems in an informative case-study format [K. Wilson, *My Garden is a Car Park: and Other Design Dilemmas*, Laurence King, London, 2017].

Integrate or give views of water

Many architects shy away from water, assuming it is inherently expensive or complicated to integrate. Charles Moore's *Water and Architecture* illustrates many ways it can be achieved successfully through a number of inspiring case studies, with beautiful photographs by Jane Lidz [C.W. Moore and J. Lidz, *Water and Architecture*, Thames & Hudson, London, 1994].

Lisa Baker's *Built on Water: Floating Architecture and Design* explores architecture that interacts more directly with water. This would be a useful reference book for anybody looking to design buildings that would sit on or adjacent to bodies of water [L. Baker, *Built on Water: Floating Architecture + Design*, Braun Publishing, Salenstein, 2014]. If you are looking to introduce water into your own garden, the Royal Horticultural Society's *Ponds & Water Features* is a great beginner's guide to this subject [Royal Horticultural Society, *Ponds and Water Features (RHS Practicals)*, DK, London, 2002].

Improve ecology and biodiversity

If you are keen to know more about biodiversity and architecture, *Designing for Biodiversity* by Dr Carol Williams, Kelly Gunnell and Brian Murphy is an essential reference text that covers almost all areas, from flora and fauna species to inspiring products [C. Williams, K. Gunnell and B. Murphy, *Designing for Biodiversity: A Technical Guide for New and Existing Buildings*, RIBA Publishing, London, 2013].

There are also a number of case studies on the WELL Building website that include biodiverse features, such as COOKFOX Architects' Manhattan offices, which have their own beehives and an edible urban garden ['COOKFOX Office New York, NY, USA', Delos Living LLC, <https://delos.com/project/cookfox-office>, 2018 (accessed 17 February 2018)].

Use nature to educate, engage and involve

The fact that four out of five children are not connected to nature was taken from a three-year research project undertaken by the RSPB [F. Gerry, 'Just one in five UK children "connected to nature", groundbreaking study finds', RSPB, <http://ww2.rspb.org.uk/about-the-rspb/about-us/media-centre/releases/355947-just-

one-in-five-uk-children-connected-to-nature-groundbreaking-study-finds->, 2013 (accessed 21 February 2018)].

As set out in this book, nature can be an incredibly powerful tool for learning and developing skills. This in turn has many knock-on benefits such as improving self-esteem, self-confidence and even happiness. As mentioned, the Edible Bus Stop (a landscape architecture and design consultancy) have completed a number of inspiring projects illustrating how empowering working with nature can be ['Welcome to the Edible Bus Stop Studio', The Edible Bus Stop <http://theediblebusstop.org> (accessed 17 February 2018)].

Vitamin N: The Essential Guide to a Nature-Rich Life is a book written by Richard Louv to combat what he calls 'nature deficit disorder' in modern society. It is full of ways to integrate nature into everyday life, such as 'Create Your Own Nature Gym' and how to create a 'Nature Rich School'. It is a handy guide for designers and laypeople alike [R. Louv, *Vitamin N: The Essential Guide to a Nature-Rich Life*, Algonquin Books, Chapel Hill, 2016].

If you are interested in how to grow food in urban environments, there are a number of books available on this topic, such as Alex Mitchell's *The Edible Balcony* [A. Mitchell, *The Edible Balcony*, Kyle Cathie Ltd, London, 2010] and Chris MacLuckie's *The Urban Edible Gardening Guidebook* [C. MacLuckie, *The Urban Edible Gardening Guidebook: Your One Stop Guide to Growing Food in Small Spaces*, 5000 Miles Press, Rockingham, 2017]. These vary in style and level of technical information provided, so it may be worth investigating which is best suited to you and your project.

AESTHETICS

The analysis of happiness in five major cities mentioned in this chapter's introduction refers to a paper titled 'Untangling What

Makes Cities Liveable: Happiness in Five Cities'. This report analysed statistics about happiness gathered in each city, and found that living in an aesthetically beautiful city is one of the easiest ways to attain happiness [A. Goldberg, K. Leyden. and T. Scotto, 'Untangling what makes cities liveable: happiness in five cities', *Proceedings of the Institution of Civil Engineers – Urban Design and Planning*, 165(3):127-136, <https://www.icevirtuallibrary.com/doi/abs/10.1680/udap.11.00031>, 2012 (accessed 17 February 2018)]. Alain de Botton writes of the importance of aesthetics in his fascinating book *The Architecture of Happiness*, arguing, 'of almost any building, we ask not only that it do a certain thing, but that it looks a certain way'. De Botton taps into the idea that we have inherent mental images of how a certain type of building should look, and that if a building's appearance does not match up with our aesthetic assumptions then we find it jarring and unpleasant [A. De Botton, *The Architecture of Happiness*, Penguin, London, 2014].

Use colour wisely (and sparingly)

For a good introduction to how colour has been used historically in architecture, I would direct you again to Steen Eiler Rasmussen's *Experiencing Architecture*, where colour is discussed at some length in Chapter IX [S.E. Rasmussen, 'Color in Architecture' in *Experiencing Architecture*, The MIT Press, Cambridge, Massachusetts, 1959].

This book has only been able to touch very briefly on the impact and cultural significance of colour in design. Kassia St Clair's *The Secret Lives of Colour* provides a detailed history of each colour, as well as the science behind how we understand and interpret colour itself, and is recommended for anybody with an interest in colour theory [K. St Clair, *The Secret Lives of Colour*, John Murray Publishers, London, 2016].

If you are looking for a more design-led book on colour, David Hornung's *Colour: A Workshop for Artists and Designers* is a very useful resource on colour theory and the history of colour in art and the creative industries [D. Hornung, Colour: A Workshop For Artists and Designers, Laurence King, London, 2012].

The fact about blue streetlights being used in Tokyo to reduce crime and suicides was taken from an article in the *Seattle Times* [*The Yomiuri Shimbun*, 'Blue streetlights believed to prevent suicides, street crime', *Seattle Times*, <https://www.seattletimes.com/nation-world/blue-streetlights-believed-to-prevent-suicides-street-crime>, 2008 (accessed 17 February 2018)], and the fact about colour impacting the effectiveness of drugs was taken from the study 'Effect of colour of drugs: systematic review of perceived effect of drugs and of their effectiveness' [A.J. De Craen, P.J. Roos, A.L. de Vries, J. Kleijnen, 'Effect of colour of drugs: systematic review of perceived effect of drugs and of their effectiveness', *BMJ*, 313(7072):1624-6, <https://www.ncbi.nlm.nih.gov/pubmed/8991013>, 1996 (accessed 17 February 2018)].

Create moments of joy

One of the finest architecture books for conveying the sense of joy that light and space can produce is *In Praise of Shadows* – an essay on aesthetics by Junichiro Tanizaki. While it focuses primarily on Japanese aesthetics, the book contains lessons that can be applied to the design of any building or object [J. Tanizaki, In Praise of Shadows, Vintage Books, London, 2001].

In a more practical sense, the *WELL Building Standard* provides advice on the importance of 'beauty' and 'delight' in creating joy and visual comfort [Delos Living LLC, WELL Building Standard Version 1.0, New York, 2014].

I would also refer readers to the work of London-based collective

Assemble Studio, whose projects often feature found or upcycled materials and are all imbued with a sense of playfulness, showing that moments of joy can be achieved at a relatively low cost.

Avoid visual monotony

One of the most interesting histories of facade design and building aesthetics that I have discovered is also in Alain de Botton's *The Architecture of Happiness*, which investigates the reasons why buildings look the way they do [A. De Botton, *The Architecture of Happiness*, Penguin, London, 2014].

Francis D.K. Ching's *A Visual Dictionary of Architecture* is a beautiful book illustrating, among other things, a range of building typologies, aesthetics and materials, and is a useful guide for anybody looking to develop their understanding of architectural aesthetics [F.D.K. Ching, *A Visual Dictionary of Architecture*, John Wiley & Sons, Hoboken, 1996].

For a more detailed scientific explanation of the importance of being 'present in the moment', I would point readers towards Diana Winston and Susan Smalley's *Fully Present* [D. Winston and S. Smalley., *Fully Present: The Science, Art, and Practice of Mindfulness: The Practical Art and Science of Mindfulness*, Da Capo Lifelong Books, Cambridge, Massachusetts, 2010].

Make buildings and their parts legible

To gain a proper understanding of what makes buildings legible, we need to understand existing typologies, as these form the basis of the psychological models we all have of how buildings should be laid out and how they should look. Simon Unwin's *Analysing Architecture* provides a comprehensive range of typologies and associated case studies, which are beautifully illustrated [S. Unwin, *Analysing Architecture*, Routledge, Abingdon, 2014].

Francis D.K. Ching's *Architecture: Form, Space and Order* also has an extremely useful section on organisational patterns, spatial relationships and hierarchy, which would be very useful for anybody looking to further understand accepted building typologies [F.D.K. Ching, *Architecture: Form, Space, and Order*, John Wiley & Sons, Hoboken, 2015].

At an urban design level, Gordon Cullen's classic *The Concise Townscape* categorises and documents the different elements we are all familiar with in Western towns and cities, helping us to develop a greater understanding of how to create legible places [G. Cullen, *The Concise Townscape*, Routledge, Abingdon, 1961].

Celebrate the simple

In his book *Happiness: Lessons from a New Science*, which has been referred to as the 'key book in happiness studies', Richard Layard explains (among many other things) that, even though people in Western societies have become richer, acquired more 'things' and made their lives easier, they have not become happier. This would suggest that expensive objects and belongings are not the key to improving our happiness [R. Layard, *Happiness: Lessons from a New Science*, Penguin, London, 2005].

Instead we should consider the writings of Leonard Koren, who in *Wabi-Sabi: For Artists, Designers, Poets and Philosophers* makes the case for simple, handmade objects, flaws and all [L. Koren, *Wabi-Sabi: For Artists, Designers, Poets & Philosophers*, Imperfect Publishing, Point Reyes, 1994].

Get the proportions right

Proportions are to some extent an entirely personal decision – we trust in good architects and designers to produce buildings and objects that 'feel' proportionally correct, and it is something that cannot simply be learned by reading a book. However, some guidance does exist.

The *WELL Building Standard*, for example, offers guidance on 'visual complexity, balance and proportion' in the design of buildings, as do the writings of Le Corbusier in relation to Le Modulor [Delos Living LLC, *WELL Building Standard Version 1.0*, New York, 2014, p. 150].

Chapter V of *Experiencing Architecture* by Steen Eiler Rasmussen also provides a thorough discourse on proportion in architecture, offering some valuable insights [S.E. Rasmussen, 'Scale and Proportion' in *Experiencing Architecture*, The MIT Press, Cambridge, Massachusetts, 1959].

ACTIVITY

Given the vast quantity of literature devoted to the impact exercise can have on us physically and mentally, I will not dwell too long on this subject here. However, I would recommend Damon Young's *How to Think About Exercise*, which examines the concept of exercise (and our relationship with it) with a philosopher's eye [D. Young, *How to Think About Exercise*, Macmillan Publishers, London, 2014]. Activity is also something the *WELL Building Standard* touches on in its section titled 'Fitness', which provides some guidelines on encouraging activity, the provision of cycle storage, and exercise equipment [Delos Living LLC, *WELL Building Standard Version 1.0*, New York, 2014].

Encourage activity

As far as I am aware, not a great deal has yet been written about how buildings can encourage their users to be more active. However, the case study shown in this book by BVN Architecture (Frasers Property Offices) is a great example of a building that encourages movement and walking to increase rates of exercise and employee interaction.

On a smaller scale, Ortraum Architects recently completed a house in Finland that illustrates beautifully how exercise can be encouraged in the home. The house contains a trapeze, a climbing wall and a netted area above an atrium, which fit seamlessly into the architecture and look difficult to resist, whatever your age! [Alyn Griffiths, 'Ortraum Architects builds forest home in Finland with a trapeze, a climbing wall and a hammock', *Dezeen*, <https://www.dezeen.com/2017/10/25/mk5-ortraum-architects-faceted-wooden-house-finnish-forest-helsinki-climbing-wall-hammock>, 2017 (accessed 17 February 2018)].

Design-in spaces for exercise

There are already many fantastic built examples of projects that integrate spaces for exercise, such as gymnasiums or swimming pools. The key is to make them as easy as possible to use, which also means not neglecting the 'servant spaces' such as changing rooms and showers. If these are undersized or unpleasant, it does not matter how nice the gym is.

Some good built examples can be found on the WELL Building case study website, such as Citi's One Bay East by M. Moser, which includes a fitness centre and gym with a holistic emphasis on 'wellness', and the Visionary office building by Jakub Cigler Architects, which incorporates a running track for staff on the roof [International WELL Building Institute, WELL Projects, <https://wellonline.wellcertified.com/community/projects> (accessed 17 February 2018)].

As stated in this book, however, spaces do not have to be expensive or complex – in fact, simpler is often much better.

Design wider streets

The research mentioned in this section into how personal space affects our brain was taken from a study called 'Personal Space Regulation by the Human Amygdala', in which it is discovered that 'a patient with complete amygdala lesions lacks any sense of personal space' but that 'healthy individuals showed amygdala activation to close personal proximity'. The study argues that it may be this reaction that regulates acceptable interpersonal distance in humans [D.P. Kennedy, J. Glascher, J.M. Tyszka, R. Adolphs, 'Personal Space Regulation by the Human Amygdala', *Nature Neuroscience*, 12(10):1226-7, <https://www.ncbi.nlm.nih.gov/pmc/articles/PMC2753689>, 2009 (accessed 17 February 2018)].

To refer again to *The Death and Life of Great American Cities*, Jacobs discusses the various issues surrounding contact and intimacy in cities in her writings on sidewalks. She argues the need for clear demarcation between public and private spaces, for surveillance, and for a minimum level of activity [J. Jacobs, *The Death and Life of Great American Cities*, Random House Inc., New York, 1993]. If we desire a reasonable level of activity but also a reasonable level of personal space, we must put forward an argument for more generous 'sidewalks'. In *Within Walking Distance: Creating Liveable Communities for All*, Philip Langdon also argues the importance of 'sociable sidewalks' and the incorporation of nature into urban life, and again presents a case for more generous pedestrian areas [P. Langdon, *Within Walking Distance: Creating Livable Communities for All*, Island Press, Washington, D.C., 2017].

Another great online reference for designing healthy streets has been produced by Transport for London (TfL) ['Healthy Streets for London', *Transport for London*, <http://content.tfl.gov.uk/healthy-streets-for-london.pdf>, 2017 (accessed 17 February 2018)].

Design for the bicycle

The impact of cycling on the happiness of urban dwellers is argued well by Charles Montgomery in his wonderful book *Happy City*, which is a must-read for anybody interested in how interventions at a city-wide scale can affect our mood [C. Montgomery, *Happy City: Transforming Our Lives Through Urban Design*, Penguin, London, 2015]. The statistic that cycling reduces the risk of death by 41% was taken from a study at Glasgow University in 2017 [L. Laker, 'It's good to hear cycling to work reduces your risk of dying. But that's not why I do it', *The Guardian* <https://www.theguardian.com/environment/bike-blog/2017/apr/20/its-good-to-hear-cycling-to-work-reduces-your-risk-of-dying-but-thats-not-why-i-do-it>, 2017 (accessed 17 February 2018)], and 'fear of being involved in a collision' being the main reason people don't want to take up cycling was taken from a TfL survey in 2011 ['Attitudes Towards Cycling', *Transport for London*, <http://content.tfl.gov.uk/healthy-streets-for-london.pdf>, 2015 (accessed 17 February 2018)]. There is a huge amount of research available on designing for cycle safety, but the Construction Industry Cycling Commission is a good starting place ['Construction Industry Cycling Commission: Designing and Building Safer Cities for Walking and Cycling', Construction Industry Cycling Commission, <http://www.cyclingcommission.or/>, 2018 (accessed 17 February 2018)]. I should take this opportunity to thank Charlie Palmer from the Cycling Commission for sharing his vast knowledge of cycle safety with me. As a general rule, when designing for bicycles, routes should be safe, direct, comfortable, coherent and attractive.

Connect to nearby facilities

Montgomery also makes the argument for ease of access to amenities. In *Happy City* he explains that the more neighbours drive (to work), the less likely they are to be friends with each other, making a compelling case for our homes, jobs, parks and play spaces to be located within walking distance – particularly given the importance of social interaction already discussed in this book [C. Montgomery, *Happy City: Transforming Our Lives Through Urban Design*, Penguin, London, 2015].

Philip Langdon's *Within Walking Distance*, as the name suggests, also puts forward numerous arguments for why it is vital that we live in places where the distance between destinations is walkable [P. Langdon, *Within Walking Distance: Creating Livable Communities for All*, Island Press, Washington, D.C., 2017].

Don't overlook spaces for inactivity

One of the most interesting studies into how design can impact happiness is a Finnish paper titled 'Converting happiness theory into (interior) architectural design missions: Designing for subjective well-being in residential care centers' [R. Steven, J. Vanrie and A. Petermans, 'Converting happiness theory into (interior) architectural design missions: Designing for subjective well-being in residential care centers', *Proceedings of the 6th Symposium of Architectural Research 2014*, 23-25 October, University of Oulu, Department of Architecture, 2014]. This investigation into spaces that support 'subjective well-being' puts forward an argument for spaces that are 'mind-arousing', 'promote self-reliancy', 'support reminiscing' and help people to 'feel mentally strong'. The authors state that they provided design advice that was intentionally vague to allow for design freedom, but this research is extremely useful when considering the design of spaces for quiet reflection, which should do all of the above.

As previously mentioned, the *WELL Building Standard* also provides guidance on designing spaces in which to 'unwind, focus and meditate', including recommendations such as the inclusion of a plant wall or potted plants, good acoustic insulation, built-in audio devices and ambient lighting [Delos Living LLC, *WELL Building Standard Version 1.0*, New York, 2014].

PSYCHOLOGY

Given that this book discusses a number of areas of design, it only touches on each of the subjects that make up its component chapters, including the psychology of architecture. The books below provide good further reading around this topic.

The previously mentioned *Architecture of Happiness* by Alain de Botton is a thorough and philosophical work on how architecture affects the way we think, and is recommended to all who have enjoyed this book [A. De Botton, *The Architecture of Happiness*, Penguin, London, 2014].

Architecture and the Unconscious is a collection of essays on how architecture interacts with the mind and psyche, and is far wider-reaching than it was possible to be in this book [*Architecture and the Unconscious*, eds J.S. Hendrix and L.E. Holm, Routledge, Abingdon, 2016].

Don't overlook the importance of storage

People seem to be waking up to the idea that tidiness can have a positive impact on our lives. What was previously (incorrectly) labelled as 'OCD' is now being seen as a way to improve the efficiency and ease of our daily routines, making our lives that little bit easier, and many books have recently been written about this subject.

A favourite of mine is *Banish Clutter Forever* by Sheila Chandra, which is based around the 'toothbrush principle' – that not even the most disorganised person loses their toothbrush, as everybody gives it an allocated 'place' due to how essential and basic brushing our teeth is [S. Chandra, *Banish Clutter Forever: How the Toothbrush Principle Will Change Your Life*, Vermilion, London, 2010]. Chandra explains how to eliminate clutter and maximise storage in each room in the house, giving a useful lesson in how we can all improve the way we use our homes.

Similar titles that celebrate tidiness include *The Life-Changing Magic of Tidying* [M. Kondo, *The Life-Changing Magic of Tidying: A simple, effective way to banish clutter forever*, Vermilion, London, 2014] and *The Joy of Less* [F. Jay, *The Joy of Less: A Minimalist Guide to Declutter, Organize, and Simplify*, Chronicle Books, San Francisco, 2016], both of which support the previously made assertion in this book that we should 'celebrate the simple'.

Provide high ceilings where possible

Beyond the advice that 'higher ceilings can improve how we feel within a space, but ceilings that are far too high will start to dwarf us', there is not a great deal more that can be written about this aspect of design.

Some guidance on minimum ceiling heights (based on the width of spaces) is provided in the *WELL Building Standard* [Delos Living LLC, *WELL Building Standard Version 1.0*, New York, 2014], but generally designers should remember to always consider their spaces in section as well as plan, and use common sense and design experience to ascertain whether the proportions of the space are suitable for its function.

For case studies, including sections of some of the most successful and well-designed buildings of recent times, Richard Weston's *Key Buildings of the Twentieth Century: Plans, Sections, Elevations* is a great resource [R. Weston, *Key Buildings of the 20th Century: Plans, Sections and Elevations*, Laurence King, London, 2010].

Celebrate the entrance

This design tip is really about the idea of designing a place that is welcoming and homely, and that makes you proud of where you live. Creating a 'sense of home' is often something architects are not actually brilliant at. When I think of homes by some of my favourite architects – Mies van der Rohe, Peter Zumthor, John Pawson – they are beautiful, but not what one would necessarily call homely.

I am therefore going to recommend a book that it seems unlikely has been referenced in many architectural texts: Ellen DeGeneres' *Home*. As well as being a successful comedian and television host, DeGeneres is a serial home renovator who is passionate about design. Her book is full of beautiful built examples of homely, personalised spaces that simply make you want to live there [E. DeGeneres, *Home*, Grand Central Life & Style, New York, 2015].

Go open plan

As discussed in the main body of this book, the idea of open-plan living is heavily debated due to the perceived sacrifice of privacy (although it is reasonable to argue that this need not be the case). However, there are now large bodies of research connecting mental health and social interaction online, and the Mental Health First Aid (UK) course teaches that social isolation is one of the key risk factors for poor mental health [Mental Health First Aid England, <https://mhfaengland.org> (accessed 12 February 2018)].

Bigger isn't always better

There are a number of books available on the subject of 'compact living', as it is growing in popularity in different parts of the world. A lovely example is *Beautifully Small: Clever Ideas for Compact Spaces* by Sara Emslie. Emslie makes a compelling case that a small space can not only be usable and liveable, but also somewhere beautiful that we would love to spend time in [S. Emslie, *Beautifully Small: Clever Ideas for Compact Spaces*, Ryland Peters & Small, London, 2014].

Consider prospect and refuge theory

The key book on the topic prospect and refuge theory is of course Jay Appleton's 1975 *The Experience of Landscape*, where he first argued that most people are inherently drawn to environments that allow us to see without being seen. It is sadly out of print now, but many of Appleton's ideas on this subject can be read online [J. Appleton, *The Experience of Landscape*, Wiley-Blackwell, Hoboken, 1975].

In the aforementioned *Happiness: Lessons from a New Science*, Richard Layard supports Appleton's theory, arguing that security is indeed one of the most important factors in our happiness [R. Layard, *Happiness: Lessons from a New Science*, Penguin, London, 2005].

Create an atmosphere

Many architects and theorists have written about architecture and atmosphere, but Peter Zumthor's suitably titled *Atmospheres* is one of the better examples, and provides an engaging architectural discourse on what really creates an 'atmosphere' in a built space. [P. Zumthor, *Atmospheres*, Birkhäuser GmbH, Basel, 2006].

Although it does not confine itself solely to this topic, Gaston Bachelard's *The Poetics of Space* is also a fantastic book that deals (somewhat) with atmosphere [G. Bachelard, *The Poetics of Space*, Penguin Classics, London, 2014].

For photographs of spaces with amazing 'atmospheres', *The Scandinavian Home: Interiors inspired by light* by Niki Brantmark is a beautiful book that I hope you will find inspiring [N. Brantmark, *The Scandinavian Home: Interiors inspired by light*, CICO Books, London, 2017].

CONCLUSIONS

The statistic that work-related stress, depression or anxiety accounted for 40% of work-related ill-health and 49% of working days lost in 2016/7 was taken from a study by the British Health and Safety Executive ['Work-Related Stress, Depression or Anxiety Statistics in Great Britain 2017', Health and Safety Executive, <http://www.hse.gov.uk/statistics/causdis/stress/stress.pdf>, 2017 (accessed 12 March 2018)].

INDEX